ISBN 978-1-330-14759-7
PIBN 10037580

This book is a reproduction of an important historical work. Forgotten Books uses state-of-the-art technology to digitally reconstruct the work, preserving the original format whilst repairing imperfections present in the aged copy. In rare cases, an imperfection in the original, such as a blemish or missing page, may be replicated in our edition. We do, however, repair the vast majority of imperfections successfully; any imperfections that remain are intentionally left to preserve the state of such historical works.

1 MONTH OF
FREE
READING

at

www.ForgottenBooks.com

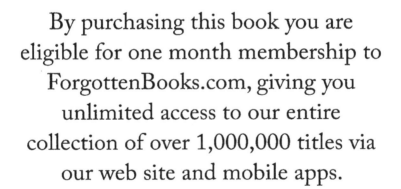

By purchasing this book you are
eligible for one month membership to
ForgottenBooks.com, giving you
unlimited access to our entire
collection of over 1,000,000 titles via
our web site and mobile apps.

To claim your free month visit:
www.forgottenbooks.com/free37580

R. W. Murphy, M. D.

Y TO THE SECRET VAULT.

tion of Man's Origin;

THE

His Present Condition;

AND

His Destiny.

BY

ERT WILSON URPHY, M.D.

SAN FRANCISCO.

1890.

1

KEY TO THE SECRET VAULT.

Solution of Man's Origin;

THE

Philosophy of His Present Condition;

AND

His Future Destiny.

BY

ROBERT WILSON MURPHY, M.D.

SAN FRANCISCO:

1890.

Prefatory.

You cannot judge of a book by its cover. "Uniforms are often masks," said Wellington. A coward may be wrapped up in a red coat with gilded buttons; so error may be bound in red morocco; deadly poison may be gilt-edged; immoral pictures, obscene thoughts, vulgar sayings degrading to the intellect, contaminating the moral nature, may be put in the most attractive forms in order to catch the thoughtless and corrupt the innocent.

All books ought to be transcripts of good minds. For in the study of the book we are studying the author of the book. We can know but little of an author save by the study of his works; critics may pronounce for or against a book in accordance with their notions or personal idiosyncrasies and the

style of the author, whether dull or dynamic, clear
or keen cut.

The method of expression has much to do both
with the popularity and value of a book.

Often the plainest and cheapest binding may
contain the treasures of long years of the best
thought of the good and great, the brightest gems
that will enrich the race and lift mankind to the
highest plain of mental and moral wealth.   The
healthy mind will search for truth as for hid
treasure, search until it find the key to the complicated lock.

The architect who embodies his thought in temple or tower, only reproduces himself in thought
forms, the beautiful and the true, and he must be
judged by the product of his own genius.   To judge
of an architectural monument the critic must have
correct perspective.   Form, light, shade and color
have fixed laws;   the laws of optics are strictly
mathematical;   hence they are immutable and not
subject to the notions of the critics;   but while
truth is many-sided there is only one point of per-

spective where the whole is seen from the stand-point of the artist.

To reach this position requires at least two things : a desire to know the truth and a surrender of all prejudice and self-conceit. Some long established dogma, or pet creed, educational bent of mind may cause such mental aberration, that the unchangeable law will seem to make the long short, the straight crooked, or the worse to appear the better reason. Truth is often mistaken for error, and error taken for truth.

Mental aberration is the father of a numerous progeny—critics, cranks, dementia, mania and madness are but normal growths of ignorance and prejudice. Mind, mad with error attacks the truth like a wounded bear in defense of her cubs. Ignorance and prejudice carry their own two-feet rule by which they measure truth and mind.

It requires more moral courage to defend the truth in the face of the multitude than to spike an enemy's battery.

Mind, giving expression to the truth is always

divinely supported; truth cannot be conquered; it may be taken prisoner and shut up in a dungeon for a while, but release will come, and it will at last triumph.

"The immortal years of God are her's."

The heliocentric system was a philosophic truth long before Descartes made his demonstration. Truth is none the less true because the majority may reject it. The multitude may mob Galileo, the priests may threaten, but the world moves on—just as the moon does though the dogs may continue to bark at it.

Some people are intellectual idolaters; moral enthusiasts; religious fanatics; they prefer to live in darkness and feed on falsehood and die from starvation, rather than to confess ignorance and retract error. Intellectual pride prefers darkness to being illuminated by obscurity with a torch in his hand.

Some, as Ephraim are joined to their idols—intellectual idolaters beyond the reach of any Evangelist; the author has written for them also. To understand a book, read preface and page without prejudice, and from the proper perspective—the stand-point of the author. Take a bird's-eye view, so as to take in the whole by seeing all the parts in their true relations.

What can we know of the parts of a temple till the superstructure is completed and the top-stone is finished ? Wait until you read the last line of the last chapter in a book before you pronounce judgment or say, Grace, grace unto it.

Every man was made to think for himself, and if he think logically and honestly he will be heard. The Author attempts a survey of an unfenced territory—Man, his spiritual origin ; present condition and future destiny.

The book is his field notes to be examined and worked up by others.

Read it, topic and page, preface and finis.

Solution of Man's Spiritual Origin.

THE BOOK OF NATURE.

"Speak to the Earth and it shall teach thee."—JOB.

The Book of Nature is a transcript of the Author himself. A record of his thought and a manifestation of his will power. The study and knowledge of this wonderful volume will bring man nearer the heart of the Great Author, and enable him to read these ancient records.

Nature not only stimulates thought, but it is the great volume which furnished thought in the purest and most beautiful forms. It is thought in the original forms of language; the symbols of thought, emotion, beauty, power; a transcript of the Divine Mind; his plans, laws and methods of work, and final design.

Job reveals a great truth when he declares that

Earth is commissioned to teach man, and reveals also the method of the Teacher. The secret key is put into man's hands, the great store-house of learning is opened, the secrets are within mortal grasp; yet nature keeps no free schools; issues no free tickets to any of her libraries of learning. "Speak," is the divine price of knowledge; interrogate; desire to know; free yourself from all prejudice; look at her truths from the right stand-point, and in the right spirit; then she will unfold her sacred scrolls, and answer your questions.

She has epics and lyrics for the poet; cartoons, friezes and sculptured beauty for the artist; points, lines, cones and motions for the mathematician; rocks, fossils, eruptions, ripple-marks and revolutions for the antiquary; plans and purposes, progress and power, under the personal control of the divine mind working out the onward march of the centuries—all in the interests of man.

These records of primeval history, written upon the rocks in sacred hieroglyph by the finger of God; these immeasurable cycles of untold ages and strange revolutions, all in the interests of man, may be translated by man, who holds the key to the secret vault.

ORIGIN AND LAW OF MATTER FORMS.

"Things which are seen were not made of things which do appear."—PAUL.

The first chapter in the history of the earth reveals a formless void ; a mass, immensely vast, yet with limits, but in great confusion, enveloped in darkness — unorganized material akin to the heavenly planets before their birth. The Divine Intelligence brooded over the shapeless mass, as a dove upon her own eggs. Atoms combined into molecules, molecules into substances. Substances took the form of gases, and gases combined into substantial forms of matter, by the law of affinities ; dissimilar atoms were wedded by a divine law of love ; particle united with particle and formed masses, and masses were formed into worlds.

The Divine Mind but gave expression to a still higher thought and unfolded a prophecy of a wider plan, when the Great Architect gave the new earth a place among the sister planets.

It had form, and he gave it motion upon its axis and in its orbit, but earth was without life ; it was

still covered with thick darkness; by an Almighty
fiat and in accord with divine law, light came and
drove away the darkness, and the vast planetary
system, complete in its mechanism, began its
mission in the interests of the higher order of
beings, man being the climax of the divine plan.

The sun, but newly created and but feeble in his
power, yet needed another force to counteract the
solar attraction.   The attraction of gravitation, or
the persistent will force of the Deity.   Without
this law of antagonism the sun would very soon rob
our planet of its vitality, but this law of attraction
is so wisely adjusted, that it restores what other-
wise would be dissipated by the sun's action, or
the earth would become parched and unfit for the
home of any kind of life.

This law of antagonism is divine in its origin
and includes in its range all forms of existence,
animate and inanimate; it is the great law by
which the onward progress of the world is accomplished, from the lowest to the highest forms of
life.   By it the balancings of nature are secured;
by it the mists are lifted up, the clouds surrender .
their treasure; and the floods are carried back to
the sea; the moaning winds, the muttering thunder

and the vivid lightning put to confusion the atmosphere, purify the earth, and prophesy of man.

Man himself is subject to the same law. He swings from one extremity of the arc to the other, till at last he settles down at the point of progress and moves forward. The next generation moves in the same way, only in a longer arc, and finds a higher resting point. One generation is sacrificed for another, as forests feed on the rich soil of their predecessors. Men are persecuted in one age and die martyrs, but the next age makes heroes of them and builds monuments over their graves.

Scientific and philosophic and religious truths are persecuted in one age and immortalized in another; laughed at and driven out of the world, then ushered in with music and banners and shouts of the multitude.

The see-saw of civilizations, nations and empires has been a forward movement over the graves of the buried past. The dead past is but the prelude of the onward future; out of the ruins of the old come the institutions of the new. Thus the majestic procession moves on to perfection. Matter and mind alike are under the general superintendence of the All-Wise.

LIFE AN ENDOWMENT.

"One indissoluble chain of affinity binds together all nature."
—HUMBOLDT.

"Give me matter, and I will explain the formation of a world; but give me matter only, and I cannot explain the formation of a caterpillar."—KANT.

The planets are a great brotherhood. Sun and earth are made of the same materials; made on the same plan; bear the same image—the Author is one. Thirteen elements principally compose the earth. Only four of these are prominent—oxygen, carbon, silicon and hydrogen are the principal material in world-building.

Professor Huxley reduces all material substances to water, ammonia and carbonic acid. Oxygen is the chief basis of the planetary worlds, being about equal to all other elements.

Who made the atom? What architect constructed atoms into worlds? Who gave the atom motion and form? Who developed it in accordance with a great plan?

"The genesis of an atom is no easier to conceive than the genesis of a planet."—HERBERT SPENCER.

Admit the existence of the atom, who or what gave it a start? Or could it move itself? Sir Isaac Newton denied that the force of gravity was in the atom, and Faraday, the greatest modern thinker on this subject, pronounces the dynamical theory absurd.

> "When nature underneath a heap
> Of jarring atoms lay,
> And could not heave her head,
> The tuneful voice was heard from high,
> Arise, ye more than dead!" —DRYDEN.

Man may not be permitted to know much about gross matter, yet he may have some insight into nature's methods and the plans of the Author of nature. Primary among his methods must be the law of affinity, that mysterious power by which heterogeneous elements are drawn together and held in their places to form gases and grosser forms of matter. Oxygen is not water; Hydrogen is not water; but combine the two in the right proportion and water is the resultant—that is, water is created or produced from that which was not water.

The methods of the Author of nature may be examined, for the law by which they are combined is exact, mathematical; it is the law of chemical equivalents. This great law gives the method of the formation of all inanimate substances; gases, rocks, metals, etc. So that "things which are seen were not made of things which do appear." By the analysis of matter we find the world is built upon mathematical law, and hence its Author is the Great Mathematician. The chemical world is built upon the laws of arithmetical proportion; the world of forms, crystals, mountains, and worlds with their motions in space, are all constructed in accord with geometrical laws; mineralogy is divine, solid geometry.

The visible world is a divine system of spheres, cubes, squares, angles, lines in motion; geometrical forms moving according to geometrical law. Here man holds the key to the secret of inorganic matter and nature-forms; but is there a key to organic forms? Will the law of affinities account for vegetable and animal forms?

THE PROCESS OF DEVELOPMENT IN VEGETABLE AND ANIMAL LIFE.

" The rounded world is fair to see,
Nine times folded in mystery;
Though baffled seers cannot impart
The secret of its laboring heart,
Throb thine with nature's throbbing breast
And all is clear from East to West."—EMERSON.

The separation of the water from the land was a physical necessity to the production and development of vegetable and animal life. Divine intelligence gives a key to his thought and great plans in the production of the lowest forms of life; the revelations of these plans are seen especially in the construction of the first forms of animal life. The fish is not the first form of man, not the first cast of the divine Artist, but it is the prophecy of the coming man.

"Man is the purpose toward which the whole animal creation tends from the first appearance of the first paleozoicfish."—AGASSIZ.

But before vegetable or animal forms could have place, the law of antagonisms must be wisely adjusted and put in force; this is a higher law than the law of combination or chemical affinity, or the mathematical law of form ; it includes the thought of force, motion and personal superintendence.

The currents of wind set in motion by solar heat, swept over the great deep, setting the waves in motion, which being resisted and curbed by the antagonizing force of gravity ; so that the mad billows, by this action and reaction were decomposed and another elementary force liberated ; that most subtle agent, electricity, which plays so great a part in the phenomena and among the forces of the world. It is the indispensable agent in the development of vegetable and animal life.

There is not an ocean wave, a roaring cataract or wailing wind that sweeps the mountain or the plain ; or wing of bird or bee that beats the air in its daily flight, but generates electricity ; every particle of this magnetic fluid is vitalized. These forces are correlated into vegetable forms of life, these agaiu into animal forms, and these into spiritual forms.

Perhaps not more than a millionth part of the sun's light and heat and solar attraction reaches our earth ; and yet these forces are so well adjusted that they are just enough to nicely antagonize the force of gravity in our planet and keep all balanced. The final result and product of these antagonizing forces is the life-giving principles; intelligence with all its wonderful pontentialities.

Sun and earth, the positive and negative agents, are working in harmony with God, the divine Intelligence and personal power operating through them by his divine law of antagonistic forces.

This law is not some force put into matter and there left to operate itself; nothing is left to blind fate; but the divine Intelligence is ever present directing the evolution of vegetable and animal life.

INDIVIDUAL LIFE FORMS.

There is a universal stamp put upon all organic being that is divine in its origin, inherent and transmissible in its history. Individuality has permanent and fixed laws, immutable through all ages; each after its own kind is the divine law of living beings. There is no accidental law. The great Author is present unfolding his plans in all vegetable and animal forms, in all the past; flower and fish, forest and family have kept their forms and preserved their habits, amid all the revolutions of time. The flowers we cultivate in garden or home continue to preserve their individuality and unfold their beauty from seeds produced years ago in other climes; the form, color and odor remain as permanent elements of character. There seem to be some exceptions both in the vegetable and animal world, which are only freaks of nature; these will be treated in their proper places.

This law of life is most remarkable and beneficial to man and divinely wise. In man it seems to blend with the different races, but only to produce another variety; the type remains unchanged.

There may be some truth in the Darwinian theory, but it is not all true. Man never sprang from the monkey or the baboon or any mere animal, but was created a separate, independent type.

Monkeys and baboons never show any moral qualities; no reverence for the Divine Being; no disposition to worship; they are not capable of any moral development; for them there is no such thing as science. These permanent, historical facts are conclusive evidence that man has a higher origin than mere animal being; that no centuries can change one type of being into another.

There may be some striking resemblance between the physical anatomy of man and some animals.

There is some resemblance between the oak tree and the walnut; but as the walnut could not come from the oak, much more man could not come from the baboon.

Man has an animal nature, but is more than an animal; he possesses a high spiritual and moral nature that lifts him above the beasts of the field and links him to something higher. Man intellectually has made great advancement; his history is one of grand achievements and great acquirements in knowledge.

His genius is seen in his inventions, in the arts and sciences, philosophy and poetry, and mechanical pursuits; bringing the elements under his control and making them serve him. He harnesses the unseen forces about him like steeds to his chariots, and guides and controls them as with bit and bridle. He measures the stars and calls them by name, and weighs the planets in his scales.

Man has moral powers unlimited in their range. Most of the animals show some capacity for a certain kind of education, but it is man's moral qualities that distinguish him from the lower animals, and make him a companion of the angels and entitle him to a Divine revelation for his guide.

He is a moral agent, free to act for himself, only limited by the laws of his own freedom; this enables him to hold communion with God and to receive a certain amount of Divine love and truth so as to mingle with his spiritual nature.

"O rich and various man! Thou palace of sight and sound, carrying in thy senses the morning and the night and the unfathomably galaxy; in thy brain the geometry of the city of God; in thy heart the power of love and the realms of right and wrong."—EMERSON.

Man has the power to unlock the secret history of the past, raise the dead from their rocky tombs and unloose the tongue of the forgotten ages. He is the head of an ascending series, the last term, the objective point in creation. For him the untold centuries have lived; atoms have been combined into worlds; flowers have bloomed and died; millions of beings have walked the earth, then have been transmuted into soils; revolutions have lifted the mountain systems; formed the valleys; cut the river channels and purified the atmosphere; all for the preparation of the human home, the complete development of the race, and to unlock the secrets of matter and mind, and bridge the gulf between life and death.

THE KEY TO THE LAW OF EVOLUTION.

" The universe is the realized thought of God."—CARLYLE.

" Mind is God's first end."—CHANNING.

" All really scientific experience tells us, that life can be produced from a living antecedent only."—UNSEEN UNIVERSE.

The universe, including man, is an evolution of God. This is the only evolution possible to thought. This world and all worlds, including all phenomena, physical and spiritual, in all detail, are but the manifestation of the invisible and personally conscious Intelligence, working out his plans according to his own methods. The great object revealed by these divine manifestations is the formation, development and destiny of man.

Development must have a developer and a law or a method of development. The machinery of the world must have a machinist and a personal superintendent.

The plan of the Deity and his divine processes are written in distinct chapters and in hieroglyph on the face and in the secret places of the earth. Great epochs mark the history of the earth, and its wonderful revolutions are but the divine processes of fitting up this planet for the abode and development of man.

The order of the divine plan as written in the earth is :

First, Atoms or essences, molecules, particles and substances united by mathematical law and held together by a divine force called chemical affinity, in the plastic forms of matter.

Second, Mathematical points about which matter centered by the force of attraction.

Third, The masses thus formed are put in motion according to mathematical law, and they assume mathematical forms.

Fourth, These masses are put in motion and kept in motion by the presence and power of the Great Intelligence.

Fifth, As the earth begins to cool, vapors are precipitated and are condensed into water and cover the face of the earth.

Sixth, The seas are joined about the globe to complete the equilibrium about the centers of motion, and the dry land appears.

Now earth is but a dreary solitude, with nothing to disturb the awful silence but the wailing winds and mad seas dashing themselves to pieces against the cold, hard rocks.

The antagonism of the waves set at liberty that subtle agent, now called electricity.

Seventh, New and more complex combinations then take place. Rocks and metals are formed, the metals crystallize in beautiful forms by mathematical law, the prophecy of higher forms.

Eighth, Another form of Divine force is introduced : the mysterious life, force, and the prophecy in the metal forms is fulfilled, and earth is clothed with ferns and flowers.

Ninth, The flower in its organic structure, produced by matter centering about this new point of attraction, the life centre, now becomes a higher grade or order of prophets to introduce a new order, and another form of Divine force.

Tenth, The introduction of animal life. Above the blooming, fragrant flower wasting its beauty on the desert air, appears the beautiful Psyche fluttering and humming the prophecy of bird and beast and man. But earth was unfitted for the abode of higher animal life. Monstrous, gigantic forms of life first appear suited to the hot and horrible climate. Trilobites, ammonites, frogs, lizzards, the huge and hungry ichthyosaurus, mastodon and megatherium, that have been preserved in their desolate graves, are proofs of the predecessors of man.

The consumption of the oxygen of the air by millions of air-breathing animals produced an atmosphere of carbonic acid gas. Seas of poisonous atmosphere enveloped the animal world, till at last the equilibrium was restored by the death of millions of these monsters. The fossil forms are found in the secret places of the earth, the history of the age engraven in the rocks forever. Gigantic forests then covered the earth on a scale with the extinct animal life, and consumed the seas of carbonic acid gas and converted them into forms of beauty and sources of wealth for the coming man.

Long ages pass; ferns grow in the dark, sequestered nooks and shadows of the trees; flowers bloom in solitude and drink in the sunlight and transmute it into shades of beauty and sweetest fragrance; busy life develops into higher forms as the atmosphere becomes purified; the old species do not change, but more perfect varieties appear; still, earth is not ready for the home of man. Great revolutions must first take place, and

long, long ages are to be employed in this great
work.

Continents are to be raised from the bottom of
the sea; oceans are to exchange places with the
land; mountain systems are to be formed; great
valleys carved out; river channels cut, so that the
home of man might be irrigated and the future
citizen might have commerce with his fellow.
Hundreds of volcanoes must open their safety-
valves; revolutions, through the agents of fire and
water, must uproot the forests and convert them
into fields of coal, wells of petroleum and fountains
of gas. Earth must be turned upside down and
inside out in order that iron mountains might be
formed and the precious metals deposited in the
secret veins of the rock; that salt might be brought
to the surface and minerals be within the reach of
man; that sandstone and limestone might be found
in the quarries for his palace and marble for his
tomb; and that an atmosphere might be formed
in which the future cosmopolitan might live and
be developed.

When all was ready, and ages of revolutions had
wrought out their mission, man appeared on the
stage of active life, not as a development of some

higher animal forms, but the top-stone of the temple; the highest evolution of God; the incarnation of spirit and soul in his own image. God is our Father, and we are his offspring and the crowning work of his hands.

The greatest work of Deity, that for which the earth itself was built, was the creation, development and discipline, and the perfection and final elimination of the human soul from gross matter. There is no process in mathematics more certain than God's method of transmuting matter and spiritualizing it for the purposes of spiritual intelligences.

The chief object in giving form and development to earth and position in the solar system was, that through the divine forces of solar attraction and the attraction of gravitation, life would be possible. By the great chemical laws established by the Divine Intelligence, being was to ascend through a long series from the lower to the higher, until the climax was attained in man, a spiritual being with an indwelling soul. This essence of the spiritual nature outweighs worlds, in value, is more important than all the planetary systems that fill the unexplored space of the universe; for man, the perfected man, will forever retain his individuality and personality, and will become a companion and co-laborer with Deity himself.

The development of spiritual intelligence is at the expense of years and revolutions in gross matter. Earth is daily growing colder and constantly changing as man advances toward greater perfection and as spiritual intelligences and spiritual potentialities increase.

"It is impossible not to believe in the children of the gods."
—PLATO.

The fact that man believes in a higher order of intelligences is proof of man's own power. The history and revolutions of the earth were the prophecy of the coming man. The ideal was perfection. He must be more than a trained and developed animal, he must be on a plain with the gods. In addition to instinct and appetite, he must have reason, imagination, conscience and will power ; he must be personal, responsible and immortal. He must bear the image of his Creator. He must be able to command the forces of nature, rule the animal kingdom, convert the mineral kingdom to his own uses. He must cut down the forests and quarry the rocks from the mountain

and convert them into cities; melt the iron mountains and shape them into instruments of husbandry
and roads of commerce; be able to harness the
lightning, bottle up the steam and turn the world
into a speaking gallery. He must be able to create
a philosophy and to answer his own questions;
solve the problems of the stars, personal existence
and human responsibility. He must have a spiritual nature and be able to commune with God.

Can such a being be created by an Almighty fiat,
or must he be developed and disciplined by the
same eternal law of antagonistic forces? Is not
character a result of conflict, the product of action
and reaction?. Does not matter affect mind and
mind modify matter, and by this great law of
forces produce personal history? The most perfect ideals of beauty and excellency lie in the
realm of developed, disciplined man, and moral
and physical causes are blended into the one complex result, character.

The philosophy of man is the test of his intellectual powers; the proof that he belongs to the
children of the gods.

The Philosophy of His Present Condition.

THE GREAT LAW OF EVOLUTION.

"Ideas go booming through the world louder than cannon.
Thoughts are mightier than armies. Principles have achieved more
victories than horsemen and chariots."—PAXTON.

"Man cannot think highly enough of man."—KANT.

The Athenians, who boasted that they sprung
from the earth, wore a grasshopper in their hair;
in these later days the grasshopper has evolved into
a monkey, and some men are still proud of their
ancestors. From the lowest vertebrate to man,
from the savage to the sage, from the philosopher
to the perfect man, are great gulfs deep and wide,
which have never been satisfactorily bridged. The
most difficult are, the distance between the mere
animal and the man, and between the savage and
the perfect ideal-man.

One class of thinkers bridges the first gulf by the

theories of correlation, organization and spontaneous generation.   Another class bridges the second
gulf by education, discipline and regeneration.   Is
there a theory that will include all ?   Is there a
gulf to be bridged ?   Does not the Divine process
revealed in the history of the earth dispose of every
difficulty ?   Can a general law be found ?

> " To read creation, read its mighty plans—
> The plan and execution to collate."

How does the Deity produce results ?   He evolves
himself into a world of life and beauty by the law
of antagonistic forces.   Life is a series of unfold-
ings through death ;   struggle and suffering and
voluntary sacrifice has been the process through
the ages ;   these bridge all the gulfs, explain all
the phenomena, account for all results.   Suffering,
toil and sacrifice account for all development.

Man had a prophetic period ;   the revolutions
through the long ages were the prelude, the an-
nouncement of his coming.   When he arrived and
began the personal, historic period he found no
new law.   Conflict, toil, sacrifice is but a new edition of the old law ;   each link in the series rises
out of the grave of its predecessor ;   matter dis-
solves, plants live, plants perish for the sake of

animal life ; the lower orders perish for the sake of the higher ; man sacrifices life for self, and he in turn is sacrificed for others.

One nation perishes at the hand of another, but from the graves of the dead comes a higher civilization. There is an eternal see-saw among antagonistic forces, but there is coming out of it a forward movement, an onward progress from matter to man, from man to God. The trituration of the mountain, the grass on the hill-side, the bleating flock, the bustling, busy man and the powerful nation are the outcome of the force of Deity exerted through the antagonism of forces in nature.

By these the savage may be developed into the citizen, and political ideas are incarnated in constitutions and institutions and civilizations. Religious thought expresses itself in the form of temple and ceremony and systems of faith ; tombs and epitaphs mark the onward progress. Nature is one constant, unmistakable commentary on the law of development by conflicting forces, under the superintendence of Deity.

> " The chain of being is complete in me,
> In me is matter's last gradation lost,
> An the next step is Spirit—Deity!"

There have been five or six epochs and revolutions in the elevations and depressions of the earth; at least five complete organic revolutions among the living forms of the animal kingdoms, and more than that in the elevation of man to his present state of civilization; but the onward movement of the ages is under the same law and under the same Superintendent.

This law is seen in the oldest rocks. They were formed and developed by two conflicting forces— chemical affinities and forces of environment. These produced the granite and porphyries; syenite and greenstone and all the basalts. What marvelous shades! What infinite variety! What untold beauty and divine taste are exhibited by the Great Chemist in that far off, heated laboratory. These varieties of rock are proofs of the changes in climate going on in the first ages of the world, of the presence of the Chemist, combining the felspar and hornblende into beautiful porphyries.

He compounded the metalloids by chemical affinities and in due time heated them in his furnace and deposited them in the crevices of the rocks to cool; others he left in the form of oxides, carbonates and sulphurets, in order to develop the genius of man.

The fossiliferous rocks are the homes of extinct species, that lived in the hot climate in the early history of the earth ; the lowest orders of vegetable and animal life ; these were balanced one against the other ; the carbonic acid gas manufactured by the animal was consumed by the vegetable world. Had there been no conflicting forces, this condition of things must have remained unbroken forever, and all progress must have ceased at this point.

The Divine again interferes, and progress is onward. Earth's climate changed, the atmosphere became cooler, the balance is destroyed ; plants and animals perish and are buried in the rocks ; their history recorded, and another chapter is finished, and the world is again in a state of equilibrium. But new chemical combinations take place and gases are compounded, and heat is eliminated in the great laboratory ; conflagration breaks out, and the earth trembles ; the rocks are melted and lifted up by chemical forces ; all things are out of balance.

The earth moves on for ages, but the planet is getting cooler at every revolution ; the long cycles bring changes ; the revolution has altered the

world and buried the dead. The granite peaks cool
off and remain standing monuments of the past.
The metallic oxides have been compounded and
preserved in the lonely cliffs and secret places
among the rocks.   Gold, by the great law of
attraction, is hid away in veins and fissures, that
man might develop his energies in the on-coming
ages of commerce and higher civilization.

Thus, age after age have these antagonistic forces
been at work, producing revolution upon revolution; but under the guiding hand of the Great
Superintendent, there has been constant progress.
As the climate of the earth changed, new orders of
animals and plants appear adapted to their environment. Either the old species were miraculously
preserved or new creations took place, so the world
moves onward without a break.

Geological changes did not evolve man, but made
man possible by fitting the earth for his abode. * * *

THE KEY.

Has not all life—vegetable, animal and spiritual—a common origin?
Are there not three distinct grades of life, not flowing out of each other,
but in three distinct channels?   Is not this method of evolution the
universal and Divine law of all being?   Is it not contained in the universal formula of the profoundest man of the race?

"In Him we live and move and have our being."

THE ADVENT OF MAN.

" Connection exquisite of distant worlds !
Distinguished link in beings endless chain—
Midway from nothing to The Deity ! "

What a manifold mystery is man ! He has his origin in the dust, but he is a part of a divine plan that reaches to the heavens. There is a strong, intangible, invisible something in us that asks questions—What ? Whence ? Whither ? Wherefore ? What relation has organism to life ? life to the spiritual nature ? What is soul ? The fact that man can ask such questions is proof of his exalted nature. If he can ask them it is evident that he has the capabilities of answering them when once developed.

" Who reads his bosom reads immortal life ;
Or nature there imposing on her soul,
Has written fables."

We have traced the processes in nature from the dull clod up through the tiny plant and the highest forms of animal life to man. A being in whom is found the stamp of Divinity—

" Spirit, that lurks each form within,
Beckons to Spirit of its kin ;
Self kindled every atom glens,
And hints the future which it owes."

A personality with a capacity for an eternal progression toward the Deity; an onward, upward,
sublime movement toward the perfect and infinite
through the laws of truth and love. Man is the
highest evolution of God—higher than matter
forms, higher than plant or animal life; a distinct,
independent evolution; an image of the Deity
himself.

The process of the evolution of human life may
be traced from the foetus through all the transmu-
tations and growth to birth, and from birth, through
development and discipline to manhood and old age.

In all these changes the same law of antagonizing
forces is present. The body is for the use of the
spirit-nature. The nervous system, including the
spinal cord and brain, represents the inner or
spiritual man; this spiritual man is elaborated at
the expense of gross matter.

The net-work of the nervous system has its origin
in the fine nervous tubes, which contain delicate
protine threads which terminate in a cell formation; the very sensitive membrane that envelops
the nerve fibre becomes the inner lining of the
nerve cell; this cell contains protoplasm which is
received from the blood. These cells are both

negative and positive, and there is generated a
current in definite directions, which may be determined by the galvanometer. In this mysterious
laboratory, amid the most ethereal harmonicus
spirit-like currents, the human spirit seems to have
its genesis and the spiritual man to be secretly
elaborated by the Divine Chemist; but who can
trace "the way of the Spirit"?

"A beam ethereal, sullied and absorbed!
Though sullied and dishonored, still divine!"

In this secret chamber, the invisible workshop
of God, the man receives not only the stamp of
individuality, but that which lifts man above all
animal life and allies him to his Maker, personality.
The growth of the spiritual man from his genesis
to birth is at the expense of gross matter. In the
laboratory of animal chemistry is provided nourish-
ment for this immortal mystery until he comes
forth into a new world, helpless and dependent
upon others, yet endowed with power to transmit
his nature to posterity. Here he begins the conflict of life, for he grows, is developed and disciplined and perfected by the same law of antagonizing forces, though on a higher scale and in a
wider field.

MAN'S HISTORICAL EVOLUTION.

" The mind
Forges from Knowledge an Archangel's spear,
And with the spirits that compel the world,
Conflicts for empire."

Man from the beginning of his history moved on a higher plain of progression. Plants and animals were limited by their geography, to latitude, longitude and elevation. Man defies all climates, and climbs to all altitudes, and claims the world for his home. He developed a social and spiritual nature and usurped authority over all kingdoms, and began to write his own history. He gathered up the facts of the past and appropriated them to his own use.

Human records are but additional and more emphatic proofs of the Divine method of man's evolution. Personal interest or social affinities brought men together in groups. Communities, tribes and nations are but great social compounds bound by spiritual attractions, to be dissolved again in the presence of stronger affinities. Here we have the same law, only in a higher plain of life, that is found in chemical forms.

The date of the oldest records of the race cannot now be satisfactorily ascertained. Whether China, India or Africa is most ancient. If Moses has not given to the world the oldest records, all acknowledge he has furnished what are the most valuable to the race and the most reliable. A part of his writings is no doubt inspired, while much that he records seems to be facts and observations of his own, and information obtained from others. But whether inspired or uninspired, they are factors and forces in the evolution of human history and in the higher development of man.

When man reached the proper plain of intelligence he was divinely impressed through his spiritual faculties, that there was an Intelligent Power operating through matter, by which the world was brought into being and carried forward in accordance with a Divine plan.

This personal Power and Presence was called Jehovah. Man also received the impression that he was a spiritual being and possessed of immortality.

The first great event in the evolution of man's

history was the religious force and thought power incarnated in altars and temples of worship; in offerings and sacrifices and religious ceremonies. These offerings were not mere acts of worship, but prophecies, and shadows of a great event in the evolution of man's history. Jehovah selected the best specimens of the race to be workers with him in the development and discipline of all the peoples of the world. Moses and the prophets were chosen to carry out the plans of Jehovah concerning the history and destiny of mankind. Through them he gave to man the moral constitution of the world, the Decalogue, which is suited to the wants of men in all ages.

The best example of national evolution is found in the history of the Hebrew people; there is more historical detail given, and more marked epochs in their development.

The race to be disciplined and developed, must be set in families and organized into nations and fenced about with institutions.

The marriage contract, the Sabbath, and religious ceremonies, are essential to the highest evolution of any people.

THE FACTORS THAT MAKE UP A NATION.

" Nations are God's training schools for the development of man."
—A. J. N.
" Mind is God's first end."—CHANNING.

A nation is not a multitude or a mass, held together by some extraneous forces. A country and a flag is more than a crowd with a ballot; as a mob is not a city, so a race of people is not a nation. A nation is an organized people with powers, functions, responsibilities and a mission in the world.

Nations are born, grow, live and die; the individuals are bound together by sacred ties and spiritual affinities; when these are broken dissolution takes place. The life of one nation is sacrificed for the good of another, as soils are for greater growths.

The secret power of attraction is thought-force manifested through two agents; like the temple, God is the Architect and man the builder; God furnishes plans and specifications and superintends, while man constructs and works out the plans.

There are two essential thought-forces that hold nations in their places ; a centripetal and centrifugal force such as bind the planets into systems—

The doctrine of God as a personal, Supreme Ruler.

The doctrine of political equality and personal liberty of man.

These imply sacred days, sacred books, sacred oaths and sacred officers.   One people may build a Babel or a Chinese wall or a pyramid.   Another a temple, a Parthenon or a Pacific railroad.   Babylon, Egypt, Persia, Israel, Greece, Rome and America are all developments of distinct thoughts.

A complete history of man would include the entire history of this world and perhaps of all worlds.

"On earth there is nothing great but man."

The development of man through national training is a part of the Divine plan ; without social law and political restraints man would be only a savage ; a being of appetites and passions, full of sensuality, violence and crime, and tend to self-extermination.   This was his early history, and the Supreme Ruler followed the same plan with man as with the lower animals.   In the fullness of time the over-populated earth was revolutionized by the law of antagonism, and a new chapter in history begun; only a few of the best stocks were left to re-populate the earth; but from the graves of their fathers was to come another generation better prepared for higher development. The new race was set in families; social and religious restraints were imposed; the history of their fathers was a terrible lesson; the death penalty was enacted, and the value of life greatly emphasized.

Population was soon too great to be controlled by families alone, and the tendency to centralization would have again destroyed the race.

The law of antagonistic forces alone could provide a remedy; decentralization or death was the alternative.

THE WORLD'S GREAT CONVENTION DISPERSED.

The great population held a mass-meeting, or national convention, at Babel, and resolved to build a race-monument to bind the multitudes together. Jehovah defeated their plans and put them on the high way to a higher civilization by confounding their speech, breaking their language into strange dialects, and by the great law of decentralization which still sends the people from our over-crowded cities to the country, they were dispersed abroad, and stimulated by new homes and competition, they were preserved from the fate of a former history. Years elapse, and another forward movement was necessary. Jehovah selected from the valley of the Tigris the best specimen family that the centuries had produced.

The masses had become hero-worshipers and idolaters, and the tendency of the people was downward. God chose Abraham and his family and sent them to the best climate and best country then on the face of the earth ; for two hundred years they were under special discipline ; but idolatry corrupted them, passion, like a fountain of corruption broke forth, the strong, animal nature of this vigorous family must be crushed, and they must again be separated from idolaters and put under special discipline.

Isaac was a quiet specimen of ease and self-indulgence ; Jacob was a cunning, shrewd man, but needed twenty years of exile ; Joseph was sold into slavery ; Reuben and Judah, Bilhah and Tamar were not models of perfection. These Hebrews were the highest attainments in manhood the race had made, and they were sent to the strongest, best educated nation in the world, to be disciplined by the same law. The pendulum now swung to the other extreme.

They were made slaves, and recklessness was cured by hard work. A common sympathy in toil and suffering bound them together in one brotherhood. The constant worship of idols disgusted them with false gods and drove them to the living God for help. The learning of the Egyptians was essential to a preparation for their future life; Moses, their great leader, must be educated in the college of the Pharaohs.

Schooled in Egypt for two centuries, the Hebrews had increased to two millions. Moses was born at the right time and trained in the science of government for forty years; then sent to the mountains of Arabia to make a survey through the wilderness to the home of their fathers. He was commissioned at the burning bush in the deserts of Sinai, the mightiest man of all the old centuries.

The nation, the first great nation, was now ready to be evolved; it had a history and a leader, and a divine Superintendent.

Moses marched the people out to the wilderness

in a mass ; they stood in front of Sinai, heard the voice of the Almighty and saw the mountain quake. The people accepted Jehovah as King and received from him the three essentials of a nation : the Law to instruct, the Temple for worship, and the Shechinah, or special, divine Providence to lead them to national greatness and religious development.

The nation is now organized and worship is established, and the race has moved up in the scale of a higher manhood, yet years of discipline were needed to reach the best types of the nation ; development must come through suffering.

Moses died, but the nation lived on through years of conflict and struggle.

David, the most perfectly developed type among the Hebrews, came to the throne ; Solomon, his son, built the temple, the most magnificent monument the race has produced. The temple was a divine order of architecture ; ground plan, elevation and detailed drawings were all made by the Grand Master of the universe.

The workmen were inspired; Bezaleel and Aholiah were filled with wisdom and knowledge, to work in gold and silver and brass.

Moses could not have been produced by any other nation or at any other time. David must come from the sheep-cotes of Bethlehem and the temple must be built in Jerusalem.

THREE GREAT RACE MONUMENTS.

The grandest symbols of thought-forces found in the history of the race are the Pyramids, the Temple and the Parthenon; they mark the different phases of national evolutions, by the great law of antagonistic forces, superintended by the Divine Presence.

The Pyramids are grand monuments of religious thought, and mark the highest point made by the nation. It was not the ambition of great kings to preserve their names, that piled up those massive forms according to exact science. The highest attainment made in mathematical and astronomical science are recorded in that stone edition of civilization; there is the history of religious ideas; molecular, soul power at work down deep in the spiritual nature of these energetic, superstitious Egyptians; the most ancient monument of science, sociology and religion.

The Parthenon, the gods and temples and altars

of Athens were but physical incarnations of the nation's highest thought; symbols of the spiritual forces at work in the heart of the proud Athenian. He who could produce the most impressive picture of the incomprehensible powers, in statue or song, was immortal.

The Temple surpassed all monuments of the race in both magnificence and meaning.. It was the symbol of all that is true and beautiful and good. It was built for the visible residence of the Invisible Jehovah; a physical expression of his glory and a symbol of the still greater truth,—Man is the microcosm, the true temple, with sanctuary and inner court. The great object to be accomplished by the evolution of nations, was the higher evolution of man in the nations, that the highest types might be produced.

The symbolism of a people is their national biography. Religious ideas have been the intellectual and moral muscles that have elevated all peoples; all progress in art and science and literature is traceable to religious thought force; hence the best types of every nation are found in the purest religionist. The Greek culminated in Socrates, the Roman in Cicero, the Arabian in Job, and the

Hebrew in David and Paul. These are the marked men of the old past, the product of the antagonistic forces of their age under the Divine Superintendency.

The influences that operate in the production of a nation are both material and spiritual.

That which built the temple was chiefly spiritual; the outgrowth of thought and religious emotion.

THE PYRAMIDS ARE MAJESTIC MONUMENTS OF RELIGIOUS THOUGHT.

"Virtue alone outlives the pyramids,
  Her monuments shall last when Egypt's fall."

The Pyramids are monuments of religious thought; the great volumes in the nation's history and the key to the national character.

The force of religious ideas gave birth to every motive, quarried every stone in that mighty super structure. It is Egyptian mythology that solves the problem of the Pyramids.

Osiris was the god of the dead, the supreme god. He had himself died at the cruel hand of Typhon. The belief that Osiris would rise again from the dead and destroy his enemy, and that man was immortal, and the bodies should be preserved

till the resurrection of Osiris, stimulated them to
preserve the bodies of the dead by embalming
them, and is the solution of the strange fact of
Egyptian mummies.   The kings and great men
had money and power.   Their great life-work was
to build a tomb that would stand all the ravages of
time.   "Old Cheops" is the crowning monument
of the faith of Egypt in the doctrine of the immortality of man.   It is the great depository of
their knowledge of science and art, architecture
and mechanical skill, mathematics and astronomy.
Wrapt up in this sacred volume preserved in stone,
we have the history and philosophy of the evolu-
lution of the nation.

THE INFLUENCE OF NATURE IN THE EVOLUTION OF A PEOPLE.

"Is it not worth while, for the sake of the history of men and
nations, to study the surface of the globe in its relations to the inhabitants?"—GŒTHE,

Greece was the great intellectual world-center,
the birth-place of art and oratory, philosophy and
poetry; its evolution cannot be studied without
the study of its geography; climate and scenery
have more to do in the development of man
than has yet been dreamed of by the profoundest

thinkers. Latitude and longitude have set bounds
to the development of the race. This is an historical fact that must enter in to the problem of evolution as an essential factor. As the Hebrews were
the center of religious force, so the Athenians were
the acme of intellectual power. The Temple could
have been built only at Jerusalem on the hills of
Zion, the Parthenon only on the hills of Athens.

The great national centers were fixed by their
geography; the natural scenery of Greece is without a parallel.

"Greek scenery presents the peculiar charm of an intimate blend-
ing of sea and land, of shores adorned with vegetation, or pictur-
esquely girt with rocks gleaming in the light of aerial tints, and an
ocean beautiful in the play of the ever-changing brightness of its
deep-toned wave."—HUMBOLDT.

Athens was the outgrowth of her geography;
the most favorable locality on earth for the highest
evolution of human genius. The long centuries of
intense energy have produced no duplicate; in
these great Grecian Masters, art, eloquence, philosophy and poetry crystalized; they are still the
classics of all their successors. It was the great
commercial center and afforded "the market-place"
for the active minds of the world. Here was the
great arena of debate; the most complete, intel-

lectual gymnasium of the race. Here were discussed the mightiest problems of the human mind; and here mind made its most extensive surveys of all the field of thought, and produced the most perfect ideals of beauty and the finest specimens of literary genius yet attained by the race.

Here reason attained its meridian splendor; this incarnation of highest thought and culture remains as model for all time.

The songs of Homer, the statues of Phidias, the dialogues of Plato, are immortal. The magnificent temples and statues and altars; the Lyceum, the Academy, the Garden, the Temple of Demeter, the superb home of Polytion—the most magnificent of all was the Temple of Minerva, the Parthenon, the chief pride of the proud Athenian. These are chapters in the biography of the nation. What advance from the "giants" of Genesis to the geniuses of Athens!

What is the law of their evolution? Why the conflict of mind with mind and the influence of matter on mind? They are the result of antagonistic forces.

The Greek poets could have been produced no place else but in Athens.

The majesty of her mountains, the music of her seas, the genial sunlight, the pure breezes, the snow-capped mountains, the finely wooded hills, the olive and palm, the matted ivy, the golden crocus and blooming asphodels, were divine poems scattered broadcast, and these geniuses had only to read and translate.

Subtract the natural scenery from Grecian poetry and the beauty and inspiration are gone; it is the woof of the immortal web of their supernal thought. Byron never could have written his finest lines except under the inspiration of her splendid scenery. Attic air was a better stimulus than English brandy—

> "Yet are thy skies as blue, thy crags as wild;
> Sweet are thy groves and verdant are thy fields,
> Thine olives ripe as when Minerva smiled,
> And still his honeyed wealth Hymettus yields."

The product of Grecian genius was inspired thought-force. They were not geologists studying rocks and fossils and revolutions of forgotten ages, but poets translating the Divine thoughts in mountains, seas, birds and breezes. They were the best dreamers of the world struggling for the light; searching for God, to know his character and the powers and responsibilities of man. They saw the invisible powers back of force and energy and law; but saw through a glass darkly. They saw back of all phenomena there must be personality; and they filled mountain and stream, and forest and crag with dryad and naiad and oread; living beings instead of the abstract forces of the laboratory; the invisible, spiritual powers were their inspiration.

Conflict of the highest thought gave birth to both the nation's institutions and the national spirit. The gods of Athens, the temples and altars, her statues and philosophy, her poetry and oratory, are the growths around a common center. The statues of Jupiter and Juno, Neptune and Pluto, Minerva and Apollo, were but the highest efforts of human genius to incarnate the invisible in forms of beauty and power; back of the threatening storm-cloud and deep muttering thunder, the forked lightning and moaning ocean must be some spiritual personality.

Among the four thousand gods of Greece there was no image of the true God. Jehovah was not in the range of the highest imagination. They built a plain altar and placed upon it a public confession of the nation in the simple inscription, AGNOSTO THEO—To the unknown God. This marks the highest limit of the nation's evolution. It must have more light or perish; but it rejected the light and died, and all posterity feeds out of its richest accumulations.

THE COMPLEX FORCES IN THE FORMATION OF OTHER NATIONS.

Modern nations are no exceptions to the great law of antagonistic forces.

France is a most remarkable nation. The outgrowth of religious, political and social forces; a nation full of dynasties and dynamite, still ready to explode at any moment. It has produced at least two of the most powerful men: Napoleon and Victor Hugo; one is the product of victories and defeats; the other, a mountain of the richest ore, the result of the great upheavals of society and social life.

The conflicts of his times developed Napoleon, the most ambitious and mightiest military genius of the race. He was the greatest force of its kind ever let loose on earth; the man of destiny, disasters and defeats.

God defeated all his plans at the battle of

Waterloo by sending a rain-storm the night before the battle to swamp the great guns of the world's greatest artillerist, in order that Europe might have time to get its breath. During the dreadful pause, God pushed the civilization of the world forward a thousand years. Men perish, but out of their tombs come other forces to lift their fellows upward. Man may say—

> "I can command the lightning and am dust!
> A monarch a slave! a worm! a god!"

The evolution of Europe is the result of the literature of England, the philosophic thought-force of Germany, the gunpowder of France, and the Gospel introduced by St. Paul and superintended by a national Providence and a personal, Divine Presence.

The great central thought of the American nation is the most advanced and the most emphatic; the doctrine of *Liberty* is both center and circumference.

The rights of man have never been so well formulated or pushed to the front by any other nation in history. These are clearly stated in our bill of rights, incorporated and inwrought in our constitution and unfurled to the breezes in our flag.

The conflict necessary to maintain these principles against antagonistic forces produced our
national character; the highest type that has yet
appeared. It gave birth to our heroes and statesmen and constitutional lawyers, our capitalists and
our inventors; it cut down our forests, built our
cities, fenced the valleys, tunneled the mountains,
built our railroads, and filled the warehouses of the
world with bread. Liberty, is the magic word that
thrills the race and sends the people by thousands
to our shores. There is both Divine plan and purpose seen in the law of immigration. In the
western world, by the conflict of free thought, God
intends to solve the problems of all the centuries;
and by the great battle of ideas to eliminate error
and lift the race to the highest civilization.

"There have been more changes in thought in the last thirty years,
than since the beginning of the world."—PRESIDENT HITCHCOCK.

The Anglo-Saxon are all packing up for the
west; the tide was never so great as now. If Rome
shaped the politics of the Old World, and Greece
her literature and art; if the Jews gave to the
world a spiritual momentum, what will be the forward movement of the race when all these forces
are combined in one nation? There has been no

history so marked, none has made such rapid progress in population, wealth and civilization as America, and no people are so well fed and happy as Americans.

"America may reasonably look forward to the time when it will have produced a civilization grander than the world has ever known."
—HERBERT SPENCER.

"America is only another name for opportunity. It is God's final effort in behalf of the human race."—EMERSON.

America is built on the doctrine of a personal God, a Divine Superintendent and a Supreme Judge, and the doctrine of the political equality and personal liberty of man. It has given to the world the Declaration of Independence, free speech and a free ballot, the Emancipation Proclamation and the Fifteenth Amendment, and the highest civilization was born in a day.

The nations of the past attempted to build their civilizations on caste, on culture or on law, but all have perished. America has for her corner-stone personal liberty, the rights of conscience and freedom of speech. Ages of experience have taught man that the best method of developing the race, the great law of historical evolution, is found in the revolutionary power of ideas. America is the highest result yet reached by all the centuries.

THE EVOLUTION OF PERSONAL CHARACTER.

"Some are born great, some achieve greatness,
Others have greatness thrust upon them."
—SHAKESPEARE.

The great want of this age, both in church and state, is the study of great men. All great events center around a few great men at the centers of influence and power; hence these central characters become the greatest phenomena of history; here may be obtained some real notion of the wonderful capabilities of the human soul and its lofty aspirations.

The present century has given more study to the philosophy of human history than all the preceding eighteen, and the results have been reduced to two theories represented by Carlyle and Spencer. First, great men mould the masses. Second, great men are the product of the masses—or the query : Are great men produced by revolutions or evolutions ?

No solution of this problem is possible that rejects God as the prime factor in personal history;

God puts men in the great world-movements in his own way and in his own time.

Abraham and Moses, David and Paul, Confucius and Plato, Homer and Shakespeare, have been great centers of influence, great world-forces in the evolution of the world's history.

As the quarry is greater than the block, and the fountain is greater than the stream, so man is greater than all his works. Abraham is more to the race than all his history ; the choice man of his age was put in training under the personal direction of Jehovah. He was separated from the heathen and left their gods beyond the flood, and followed the voice of the living Jehovah ; he crossed the Jordan, built an altar and held communion with God ; he passed through great trials, high tests of loyalty, and surrendered self. Jehovah visited him at his tent, and promised him great things in the future. Abraham believed God, sacrificed his dearest idol, and thus the father of the faithful was produced. Moses is a complex force composed of great personality, the influence of his mother, the culture of the Egyptian college, patriotic devotion to his slave-people, forty years training in the desert and forty years of the personal presence of Jehovah. These great opportunities added to his own genius and personal development in the struggles with his enemies and the perverseness of his own people, produced Moses. Out of these conflicts, aided by Divine influences, came the great Lawgiver, the mightiest man of the Old Testament times.

Plato is a compound of the sayings of Socrates, the debates of the "Market Place" and the influences of the Academy; he is the sum of all philosophy; the wisdom of the race condensed in one man. Every thing passed through his mind and was colored by his genius. But his inspiration came from God; he depended on him. "If it please the God, you will make great and rapid proficiency; you will not, if he does not please." In him the Divine and human meet in the highest intellectual plain. "If Jove should descend to earth, he would speak in the style of Plato."

Philosophy is a revelation; Plato is the Apocalyptic Angel, the personal evolution of all philosophy.

But philosophy alone cannot shape the world correctly. Religious thought is the great force that has shaped the ages. As there can be but

one greatest thought, so there can be but one greatest man ; that man is Jesus.

Paul and the colleges of the apostles and the
great geniuses of the race, did for the intellectual,
social and spiritual world what the internal fires and
physical forces have done for the material world—

Fitted the earth for the highest civilizations and
the highest conditions of human development.

But there is something greater than logical argu-
ment or the ability to organize truth into a system,
something greater than preaching : it is humility,
self-sacrifice, the spiritual power of a personal life.

Jesus is greater than the whole college of the
apostles, greater than the combined genius of the
race ; he is the only perfect IDEAL-MAN.

A class of men was chosen by the Master for the
purpose of carrying out the details of the plan of
the Father for the highest evolution of the race.
Each of the twelve was a factor in the plan, each
performed his part of the work in the evolution
of truth.   Evangelism, instruction, organization,
apocalyptic vision and betrayal, are but the prime
factors of the Divine plan.

Who can determine which man played the most
important part ?   Which was the greatest moral

force ? Which has resulted in the greatest good, Pentecost, or Aceldama ?—the field of blood ; Peter or Judas ? The profession of Paul the martyr, or the confession of Judas the traitor ?

"They are but parts of one stupendous whole."

They are all in the Divine plan. "Jesus knew from the beginning who it was that should betray him." Hence he was neither disappointed nor deceived. What would have become of the kingdom had Judas not been chosen an apostle ?

The voluntary sufferings of the apostles and the agony of Judas the transgressor are the great spirit forces from the opposite hemispheres of the soul moving on together, turning the tide of human sympathy of all the future generations toward the Man of Sorrows.

This force moving forward with increasing energy must culminate in the highest evolution of the individual and the race, by the eternal law of compensation. The evolution of character is the purpose of all the Divine plans and the interpretation of all the facts of history.

JESUS IS THE HIGHEST MANIFESTATION OF PERSONAL CHARACTER.

Jesus of Nazareth is the most exalted and most complete character that has ever appeared on earth. He is the Ideal-Man that has revolutionized the thought of the ages, changed the moral atmosphere of the world and furnished the race with a perfect model for human living.

He is the Divine clothed with and dwelling in a fleshly body. He was so conscious of the indwelling of the Divine, that he said, "I and my Father are one." He is the highest incarnation of God, and a necessity for man's spiritual nature, as the grandest exhibition of love. He was promised by the prophets, and came in the fullness of time to fulfill Jehovah's pledge, sent by the Father to give a new life to the world and a higher class of teachings and miracle working for the spiritual advancement of the people, and to convince them of the truth. While Jesus is the highest type of man and the highest incarnation of God, he is not the only incarnation of the Divine; wherever the innocent babe is found and the pure in heart, there God dwells; there the Divine is incarnated. What is the new birth taught by Jesus but an incarnation of the Divine ? 'So that all thought and all purposes are changed for good.

God dwells in his prophets and ministers of all ages ; what is prophesying and preaching but God speaking through men ? This is God's method of giving expression and exposition to his own revelation ; so that every one conscious of the Divine truth and love in the heart can say, I and my Father are one.

The same Divine Spirit that filled to overflowing and illuminated the great soul of Jesus and made him the willing sacrifice for the good of others, fills man's spirit ; it supported the martyrs in their unfaltering tread to the stake. The teachings of Jesus are the thoughts of Jehovah and ought to be accepted by all because they are the very best the race has.

His Spirit is the sublimest exhibition of purity and love. He was led by the Divine Spirit to be tested in the wilderness, and voluntarily surrendered himself to die on the cross ; he could not refuse the Father, and was sustained by him ; he accepted the work his Father gave him to do, and sealed it with his blood.

Whether Christ died to redeem fallen man or for

a principle or doctrine that if obeyed would save man, matters not, so far as our responsibilities go. Christ could not have done more than he did to save ten thousand worlds.

God gave the Messiah to the world, and Christ is the Saviour of all who accept his doctrines and live them.

Jesus is the universal mind, the highest expression of humanity; there is no teacher like him; in the range of his thought he surveyed both worlds; in his method he is alone; he never learned letters, belonged to no school of philosophy, no sect in religion; he compassed all the race. While a Jew by birth and early influence he was broader than Moses or Abraham, broader than Brahmanism and all the old religions of the world.

Confucius was a great teacher, but he was only a Chinaman; Chinese in thought and expression, and limited by the boundaries of his own people. Plato was a great teacher, but he was a Greek; he was limited to speculative science; his method was dialectic, his spirit was Greek; he organized no schools, built no temples, left no systematized thought, has no disciples.

Paul, the highest development yet made by the race, was only the great disciple and expounder of his Master; he never added a line to the teachings of Jesus. Paul has 'no school and no disciples. Jesus is the Universal, Ideal, Perfect Man; the mightiest of all the ages and the model for all men; not a man, nor the man—but *Man.* "An Israelite, indeed, in whom there is no guile."

Sublimity of character, immaculate life and spiritual power are the Divine forces incarnated in Jesus, which will conquer all antagonistic forces and draw all men unto him.

"Jesus has no visions; God does not speak to him from without. God is in him; he feels that he is with God, and he draws from his heart what he says of his Father. He lives in the bosom of God by uninterrupted communication; he does not see him, but he understands him without need of thunder and burning bush like Moses, of a revealing tempest like Job, of an oracle like the old Greek sages, of a familiar genius like Socrates.

"Complete conqueror of death, take possession of thy kingdom; whither shall follow thee, by the royal road which thou hast traced, AGES OF WORSHIPERS !!"

—Renan.

EVOLUTION THROUGH SUFFERING.

Disease, decrepitude, disappointment and death are great facts full of mystery. Who shall furnish a key to this sad secret?

Epicureans have taught for ages that the good overbalances the evil and that this is the best possible in a world of matter.

Idealists have said that poverty, misfortune, affliction, strikes and bread riots are only the poetry of life; but suffering for the right, or moral sacrifice, is the philosophy of moral development, a method of the evolution of character and the highest moral force in the universe.

To get the flour out of the wheat, it must be ground between the upper and nether millstones and be bolted; to get the gold out of the quartz, it must be crushed before the gold can be separated; so the highest qualities of manhood are often developed through suffering.

The crust of the globe is mostly made of animal remains. Our richest soils which produce the golden grain, the most luscious fruits and fragrant flowers, are but the dust of the graves of dead generations; our limestone ledges and sandstone hills, and our beautiful oxides which are decomposed by the storms and triturated by the years into the most productive soils, are only the sacrifices of the by-gone ages transmuted into valleys of wealth for the personal benefit and higher development of the race.

These apparent contradictions are not accidents; God makes no mistakes; they are parts of a divine plan for the complete development and highest perfection of man.

Earth is full of calamities, accidents and catastrophes on every page of its history. Earthquakes swallow up whole cities, and hundreds of thousands of lives and millions of money are destroyed. Hundreds of frightful volcanoes vomit forth destruction and floods of fire overwhelm the horror-stricken inhabitants; the desolating tornado and terrific cyclone, physical monsters without mercy, rush in wild fury, powerful and pitiless in their work of death. Is there a defect in the planetary system? Have the physical laws broke loose from the Great Superintendent? No! Emphatically no!

Drouth and famine stalk abroad with haughty
step like fiends, lawless and invulnerable, and
whole countries are reduced to starvation. Epidemics, with silent tread steal into the homes of
poverty and wealth, and neither science nor sacrifice are able to explain or defeat the terrible
scourge. Is the Superintending Power unable to
control his own work, or is man ignorant and unable to explain ?

There are freaks in nature in the forms of
the vegetable and animal world that seem to be
difficult to explain—strange defects, mysterious
malformations, unaccountable deformities. Dwarfs
among the grasses, poison among the most beautiful flowers, rot seizes a whole crop of potatoes on
which helpless children depend for bread, rust
attacks the wheat and the price rises above the
pockets of the poor, and thousands go hungry
while the warehouses of the world are full. The
cattle die from diseases and bleating flocks perish
from drouth. One half of mankind die in infancy
and a large proportion are born blind and deaf and
deformed. As the trees in the mighty forests are
crooked and gnarly and twisted and defective at
the center, so men are diseased and deformed, both

in body and in mind ; some idiotic and not able to take care of themselves, and but few come up to any correct standard of physical perfection.

There are also some examples of the wonderful intellectual capabilities of man. His wonderful achievements in the arts and sciences, in bringing the elements into subjection and using them for his own purposes. He can weigh the planets, estimate their distances and calculate to a second their wonderful revolutions ; but what a large proportion are low in the intellectual scale, with but little capacity for education, and how few come up to any reasonable standard of perfection ? Are they failures ? Then, who is to blame ? Is there anybody to blame ?

Had man the key to this mystery, would not all be plain ? But defect and error and discrepancy are found in every thing about us ; it abounds in man's moral nature.

Man has capability to hold communion with God ; how beautiful and complete he is in moral excellence and grandeur, as seen in his works of love and charity and deeds of self-denial. But how few indeed have a well developed moral character. The masses are immoral, deceitful, revengeful and treacherous; how many are dishonest, selfish, licentious and criminal ?

God looked down from heaven and saw that there was none good, none that came up to the Divine standard. What a verdict for the Creator to pronounce upon his own children! Are men failures? Has God made a mistake in bringing man into being ?

Why this imperfection in all things about us? There is nothing that seems complete. Even the revelation that God gave to man seems full of imperfections. Why a hundred different creeds, all purporting to be based upon the same revelation ? And what has been more violent than the collision of creeds ?

One claims infallibility, claims that Christ delegated all power to St. Peter and his legal successors, and hence there is no salvation outside the confessional and priestly absolution. Another limits salvation to a class called the elect, foreordained before they were born; and still another sets no limits and claims from the same revelation universal salvation of all men.

Then, there seem to be contradictions in the statements made in the Bible. David is declared to be a man after God's own heart, yet he murdered a man by putting him in the front of the battle, that he might get his wife. Abraham had his Hagar, an Egyptian concubine, and Jacob was a polygamist. Why this conflict of life and law? Why are such examples, with a hundred others, spread upon the divine record? . Choice men have their faults, and this world is one of apparent defects and deficiencies in every department.

Both matter and spirit are imperfect in their present condition; crystals are defective, the vegetable world dwarfed; animals deformed and men depraved; nations are at war, and states are in commotion politically and socially; there is a general ebb and flow in society, like the tides in the ocean; now a community is lashed into foam, then the breakers become quiet and the waves return, but to repeat themselves again in foaming white caps. Our social and political problems are the most important that ever agitated or convulsed a nation.

The race problem is not yet settled; it is liable to throw the nation into spasms at any moment. We have overworked the doctrine, that all men are born free and equal; the fact is, there is no such

thing as equality among men. There are certain
fixed laws in social life, as fixed and immutable as
in mathematics or mechanics; these must not be
violated. ·There can never be peace in·society till
some platform is discovered broad enough to com-
prehend and provide for all the wants of every
individual; any effort to solve the problem upon
the hypothesis that all men are equal factors in the
intellectual and social unit, will ever be fruitless
because it is false.

Nature has a kind of aristocracy in the intellectual and social world; a few men have always
done the thinking and planning for the many. But
the many have political rights which must be kept
inviolate; life, liberty and the pursuit of happiness belong to man by virtue of his manhood;
neither ignorance, poverty nor color can rob man
of rights which are inalienable; yet such is the
condition of society, that conflict will go on, but
the result will be the constant uplifting of the
masses.

The tendency to centralization in wealth keeps
up a constant conflict with the masses of the
people. In a government like ours this conflict is
to be dreaded by the nation; for where the great

political parties are so nearly balanced the parties may be corrupted by the money power and the state suffer great loss ; already the shadows are on the wall, and coming events are near at hand.

Labor must be better protected, monopolies must be better guarded, and personal aggrandizement at the expense of honest toil must be corrected, or all hope of adjudication may as well be abandoned. The men who work must receive their share of the profits of their own skill and labor ; their rights must be made secure or the seeds of revolution will grow, and strikes and mobs and lawless outbreaks will continue, till capital will be compelled to surrender for its own protection.

Public opinion is a bodiless spirit and cannot be controlled ; it becomes incarnate in the crowd and walks the street with fearful tread, armed with club and faggot, and in moments of excitement often reduces years of toil to smouldering ash heaps.

The remedy for this dread evil will not be found in the dreams of socialists or the inflammatory harangues of demagogues.

The real point of adjustment is the division of profits. The state needs a fixed standard by which to divide the profits between labor and capital by the law of equivalency; this is the pith of the problem. There is a master mind needed in the field of political economy; the man who will show the world some universal principle by which to determine the ratio of capital to labor, will be the peer of any of the world's great benefactors and be able to put to rest this dangerous question.

We have conflicts of religious opinions that lie deeper below the surface, but as real as the first rumbling of the earthquake or the trembling of the volcano. The time is approaching when the American people at least will protest, against any foreign power dictating in the affairs of our nation.

But a greater conflict stares us in the face; it is the legalized liquor traffic. The thought is humiliating, that a great government like ours, complaining of a surplus in her treasury; a government that has made such costly sacrifices to maintain the principles of liberty, should be a party to the collection of revenue from the nefarious liquor traffic.

A nation that has spent a billion of dollars and has sacrificed a million of her citizens in the defense of liberty, has consented to furnish the shackels and the authority of law to bind her own people in a worse bondage than bodily servitude;

a bondage which means separation of husband and wife, parents and children, and confiscation of property without any prospect of compensation.

For a government to legalize such a traffic, is to surrender its most sacred powers committed to it by its own people, to poison its own ballot-box, to corrupt the fountain of good citizenship, and to usurp the authority delegated to it by its own citizens.

A traffic, worse than the slave trade, filling asylums and prison cells; ruling society with all the terror of a despot; outstripping the savage in his most fiendish acts of barbarism; sapping the vitality of the nation, and if not checked it will shake the very foundation of the mightiest republic. It is opposed to liberty of thought, to culture and refinement, and to all moral and religious development; its influence extends from one extremity of the nation to the other, a withering curse, blighting the hopes of the future.

To save our flag and keep it floating among the nations; to save our sons and daughters from disgrace and ruin, the appeal must be to legal, constitutional prohibition, to Congress, to state legislatures, to every party and church creed, and more than all and above all, to the God of nations.

Cato desired that he might die when he anticipated the death of Rome; the wisest and best men are alarmed at the social monsters of the nineteenth century. This whiskey monster is not a dream, not a prophecy, but a fact, a real monster; not an apocalyptic vision, but a live, enormous, modern megatherium, with appetite enough to swallow the nation and destroy the race.

Constitutional prohibition must march to the field of conflict; this divine law of antagonism is the only remedy; the nation's safety demands it, and the people will sustain it; the old flag must be preserved, and the sons and daughters of the nation must be protected from this prince among the destroyers.

SUFFERING—PERSONAL SACRIFICE IS A METHOD OF THE HIGHEST DEVELOPMENT.

Personal suffering has ever been the great problem of the sages, and philosophy has failed to solve it. Is there a key? Among some of the highest order of genius it is still an open question.

Goethe, in his "Faust," gives it up, sells out life to the fiends, lives in sense, and emigrates to Pandemonium.

Shelley, in his immortal "Prometheus," sends

Misery to the market to buy bread. "Festus," the most marvelous among the recent poems, gives all men a second chance in another world. Job, the broadest and most philosophic of all the poets of the race, makes compensation, or the law of equivalence, the solution of the problem of suffering.

That suffering is one of the Divine methods of evolution, and that the law of equivalence is a Divine law, seem to be true, and may solve the moral side of the problem; but the present environment is an essential factor and must be included in order to meet the whole question.

The death of animals can have nothing to do with "Prometheus" or Pandemonium; animals lived and died for the benefit of man; and the compensation, by the law of equivalence, is seen in the rich soils that are formed out of their remains, to be transmuted into bread for civilized man. The poisons concentrated by chemical forces to form the brilliant colors of the beautiful flowers that bloom and perish in a day, are not wasted, but recompounded by the tireless butterfly and happy humming-bird into matchless motions and extatic delights. Earthquake, volcano, tornado and cyclone are but safety-valves to prevent the earth from rending in pieces and becoming uninhabitable; a Divine method of restoring the equilibrium in the imperfect condition of the globe.

Famine, born of drouth is but the prophecy of plenty that will come in due time by the law of equivalence.

Epidemics, when understood are but lessons in the laws of health that will result in greater happiness; the very best that is possible in the present condition of things.

Freaks in nature and in human nature may still lie outside our knowledge of physical and spiritual laws, but they also are under the general law of equivalence.

The gnarly oak, the deformed horse and the idiotic child now lead to the more astute study and extensive exploration of the laws of matter and life, and the results are evidences of compensation. Moral laws are more complicated than physical or intellectual, for the spiritual universe is not within the range of scalpel, or microscope, or laboratory; and revelation, from which man may expect perfection, seems to be full of imperfections and is no exception to other phenomena; but the law of equivalence is found in the facts revealed, that the

most exalted characters of history have been imperfect, so that man must look beyond for the
perfect Ideal-Man.

Creeds are the outgrowth of imperfect character,
but their antagonistic force has lifted the race
higher at every movement. Modern Europe, built
on priestcraft and caste, swung backward to skepticism and spiritual death, but the noble spirits
struggling for free thought and a higher manhood,
sailed west in the *Mayflower*, and built a new nation,
and opened the way for the higher civilization.

The Jews were the best developed and best disciplined among all the nations; they were the product
of the best stocks and long years of suffering; they
furnished the world with a class of teachers, law-
givers, statesmen, historians and poets, unequaled
in the history of the race; they still maintain
their racehood; their character is the result of the
momentum obtained from their spiritual training.

Religious forces and antagonistic faiths are only
means to ends; even the most extreme notions are
methods of the higher development of man, and
factors in the greater evolution of truth.

When Rome became corrupt, a Voltaire set all
Europe ablaze with his magic pen, and skepticism

became an epidemic. But Luther wrote a thesis that revolutionized the thought of the century, and the pendulum swung back and left Europe on higher spiritual ground.

An Ingersoll, with the powers of his musical voice may attack Christianity in the public halls of the nation and get the ear of the crowd, but the great law of antagonism will give birth to some Father Gleason, who throttles his adversary with a giant grasp, and the platform gives way before the pen, and the people are lifted upward by the battle of free thought. Materialism drives all spiritual being out of the universe, but spiritualism opens the doors and

"Thousands of spirits walk the earth, both when we sleep and wake."

Honest strugglings are the only stair-ways to a higher life; every good man suffers for his fellows, for men are evolved as statues from the block, by mallet and chisel. Could we analyze the great and good, we would find two great factors, self-denial and personal sacrifice, united by a spiritual force. The best men suffer most, for suffering is a necessity to the highest development. The death of Lucretia expels the Tarquins from Rome; the sacrifice of Virginia by her own father overthrew the Decemviri; if truth lives, a Socrates must drink the hemlock; if the Gospel be planted in the household of the Cæsars, Paul must be beheaded; if liberty be proclaimed to the captives, the president must die a martyr.

The law of equivalence pervades all life, and the price of the evolution of character is suffering.

Jesus was made perfect through suffering, and is no exception to this great law which is universal. The greatest power of Jesus is not in his wonderful teachings or his miraculous works, but in the purity of his life, his love for the race as seen in his voluntary sacrifices. Gethsemane, the court of Caiphas, Pilate's hall, and the Cross on Calvary, are the birthplaces of his power. The law is universal—perfection through suffering.

MEDICAL SCIENCE AND EVOLUTION.

As man began to multiply upon the earth and diseases and sickness began to prevail, a knowledge of the science of medicine and skill in healing became necessary for the better preservation of life and health; this necessity gave birth to medical schools and developed skill in the profession.

Medicine, the healing art, is older than the tables

of stone, and stands side by side with the Ten
Commandments in the preservation and evolution
of man. As the race multiplied upon the earth
disease and sickness prevailed ; the effort of human
genius to relieve suffering and prolong life resulted
in the development of the science of medicine.
The great school at Heliopolis had its medical
department, centuries before Moses received the
Law. Æsculapius was born at Epidaurus and
educated at Chiron, where he was instructed in the
healing art. He visited the school at Heliopolis,
then returned to Athens full of zeal and inspiration, where he lectured and practiced medicine for
many years, classifying and naming the various
diseases. After his death they erected a temple at
Athens to his memory ; hung up in the temple, in
tabulated form, were the names of the various
diseases he had classified ; any who were sick went
into the temple, pointed their finger to the name
of the disease, raised their hand, invoked the
departed spirit of the inspired healer, and were
cured. The Greeks believed he was divinely inspired and could raise the dead.

About six hundred years later Hypocrates,
called the father of medicine, was the head of

the medical school at Coan ; here medical knowledge began to crystalize in scientific form ; the light from the classic hills of Greece began to shine, and many of his writings are still found in our old libraries.

About six centuries afterward Galen was born at Pergamos ; he developed as a star of the first magnitude ; at the age of seventeen he became a devout student of medicine and finally established himself at Rome ; he was an ardent disciple of Hypocrates, and his teachings held almost universal sway till about the middle of the seventeenth century. Medical science soon began to take root in Germany, France and England ; in due time America became the equal of any nation both in medical science and medical literature. Colleges have been established, lectureships endowed, and men of great learning and intellectual force have crystalized the medical thought of the world into a science. Medical science has pushed its way into Japan, Australia and India, until the science circles the globe to bless man physically, mentally and morally. It furnishes an example of development through suffering. The great law of evolution again comes to the front. The suffering of the race evolved the science of medicine, which in turn relieved the sufferin race prolon ed life and increased the mental and moral possibilities of man ; this is the Divine method in the development of mankind.

SLAVERY, EMANCIPATION AND DEVELOPMENT.

The law of evolution through suffering and through antagonistic forces is most emphatic in the African problem ; here the elevation and development of a race of despised people is to be accomplished by the same Divine process, the law of compensation ; suffering is the one method of emancipation. As the centuries of toil and hardship made Israel the most complete and compact nation among men, so American slavery under the Divine Superintendent will raise the entire African race to a higher plain. It was the active operation of this law that brought the thousands of Africa's sons to till the soil of America. Though held as bondmen and bought and sold as cattle in the market, their condition was at least no worse than in their own native land, dwelling in darkness and superstition. To be a slave is not worse than to be a savage. For more than a century they have been schooled in industry ; they have worked in the very shadow of free thought ; the arts and sciences have been their companions in the cotton fields ;

they have breathed the atmosphere of human freedom and enjoyed to some extent the blessings of
Christianity; they have had a home training in
the best government in the world; and this system
of slavery, that has been so much abused, will prove
by the law of compensation to be the greatest
blessing to the African and to Africa, that God
could devise. They are emancipated just at the
proper time, by a law of evolution; antagonistic
forces are developed and let loose, and emancipation becomes a political necessity; politics and
and morals coincide at least once in a century
"The Dark Continent" was explored by the immortal Livingstone and Stanley, and the curtains
of the future raised, just at the time when students
in the colleges of the Freedmen are being educated
by the thousands. Sitting under the trees of the
college campus are the future railroad kings and
merchant princes, bankers, educators, evangelists,
and civil engineers and legislators of "The Dark
Continent."

The antagonism between the races will soon
colonize the American negro in his own land and
among his own people, to lift a continent of savages
to the highest civilization. These bondmen of the

past will go as freedmen of the present, not naked savages, but cultivated men; educated by the same nation that enslaved them, by this law of compensation under Divine direction.

They will take with them the principles of free government and the arts and sciences, and the Christian religion, and through these agencies a republican nation of free men will be evolved from a benighted Paganism; Africa is destined to become one of the great nations of the world.

As the brightest and purest diamonds are found in Africa, so will the brightest and purest minds be found among the sons of Ham, who once taught and ruled the world. America will be proud in the near future of her dark sons she has educated and sent forth to plant a new nation.

The United States is a stronger and better government than would have been possible had slavery not existed. The emancipation of the negro was the emancipation of the nation. Our national influence, power and prosperity are without a parallel in the history of the race. Evolution through suffering is the eternal law.

The Divine plan for the development of man may be seen not only in the physical changes going on in the earth, but in the growth of modern nations and the more recent forms of religious thought and scientific development among men.

In the wide range of religious opinions which lie between Catholicism and Protestantism, though often in apparent conflict, yet the outcome of all the antagonisms is, progress and human development; even spiritualism and the Salvation Army, extremes among the extremest, are but factors in the problem of race-development. Error serves to better define truth, and discord is but a form of revolution to lift man to a higher plain.

While perfection is not yet attained, there is constant progress, and Jehovah is doing the very best possible with the physical environments that set limits to the development of the wonderful powers of the race. When creeds and religious notions become illumined by Divine truth, and love takes the place of selfishness, the world will move forward with untold progress and man be elevated in accordance with a Divine plan.

Modern nations will be at peace, the Jews will return to Jerusalem, and there will yet be a Holy Land worthy of the name; the Temple and the Holy City will be rebuilt, and the chosen people of

God, after centuries of suffering, will reach a higher state of perfection than would have been possible without these long years of training.

Discipline is essential for the nation and the individual; both must be schooled in the hard facts called history. History is a record of the Divine processes of elevating man in accordance with a fixed plan.

The process seems slow; but the on-going years of God are not to be measured by man's chronometers. Progress cannot be estimated by the almanac.

Sometimes centuries pass with but little, apparent progress; then a nation is born in a day. History is neither an arithmetical nor a geometrical progression; its movement onward is ethical.

Man's progress depends upon two independent factors—man's environment, which is the constant force exerted, and man's will, which is the ever varying factor in character.

The events of the past cast their shadows into the future; the law is the same, hence history ever repeats itself.

Arabia will receive new light, and the dark places of the oriental world will be illuminated, love bind the race in one universal brotherhood, and God be all in all.

III.

The Key to the Secret Vault.

The mysteries of the antagonistic forces in the world's history have never yet been satisfactorily unraveled; the distinction between antecedent and cause, consequent and effect, has not been recognized by many theorists; though the terms are intimately related, the difference between them is very great. How are physical phenomena related to moral causes? Is there a key to this mystery?

The great revolutions in public opinion, the moral upheavals of history, the rise and fall of empires that make up the biography of a nation's life, and the physical cataclysms in the geological world, are not the product of moral causes, but the results of physical environment; results that follow as consequents and not as effects; the design of these results by the Moral Governor is to produce moral development, and the tendency of all this mysterious phenomena is, to develop the highest powers of man.

It is difficult to root out an old prejudice, which has been honored and petrified for ages, when error is so nearly related to truth. If man's physical environment will best account for his present condition; and disaster and violence, which are written upon the rocks and experienced by nations and individuals, should prove to be God's method of human evolution and moral development, instead of consequences of personal transgression; then what would be lost by the rejection of an old theory?

Is the song of Milton, that introduced

"Death into the world and all our woe,"

to continue to rule the faith and mould all the generations? Grant that man was created upright and pure, a free moral agent with only a test of his loyalty needed to complete his character; and suppose he should fail and suffer the dreadful penalty, does it follow that all the revolutions and catastrophes of earth, volcanoes, cyclones and earthquakes, ruin and devastation and destruction of life are the results

"Of that forbidden tree"?

The earth was made for the children of men, according to a Divine plan; there is no such thing as accident or chance, and how could the mere creature upset all the plans of the Creator which had been matured for ages before man made his advent?

If man was pure, then why should he commit so terrible a deed? Grant that man is free and subject to temptation, and peccable; he can only be free within the limits of the laws of freedom.

For God to create a being equal to himself is absurd; this were to duplicate himself, which is self-destruction. Man must be a limited moral agent under the direction of the Creator; for the facts of revealed history are the best expositions of the secret, mysterious laws of spiritual being, and they show that God does interfere with man's moral agency. For if the Divine Governor could harden Pharaoh's heart in harmony with human freedom, why not restrain man from committing so direful a deed? Man was without experience, and needed help; why was it withheld? Does not this solution of the problem of suffering and violence lay the blame upon God rather than man?

But suppose it to be true, what have the unborn

millions to do with the disobedience of Eden ? They were not there, and could not be parties to the transaction. Whatever may be the beliefs of men, the facts remain ; there is at least some other disturbing factor needed to account for the physical and moral history of the earth.

Why debate the question, which wave washed the shell upon the beach ? Does opinion change the character of the strange beauty or the place it shall occupy in the cabinet ? A phenomenon is not always the result of a cause ; it may be a method of development.

The true key to the mystery of suffering and violence must accord with all the facts, and make God supreme and good, and place man at the head of creation as the great climax of God's plans.

Man is a creature of environments ; earth, his present home, is a spiritual gymnasium, the training school for a higher state of being. Suffering and toil, disappointment and death, are not penalties, but the Divine methods of spiritual development.

The revolutions in the early history of the globe, the devastation and death of plants and animals, are but God's methods of preparing a home for

man ; the seas, lakes and river systems ; the mountain ranges, the great valleys and distribution of the
continents, all show a wise plan and unity of design,
all in the interests of man. Facts prove that there
has been more happiness and enjoyment than
misery and suffering. So that the Supreme Being
is both wise and benevolent. The structure of the
earth, and all the plants and animals that have
appeared in the distant past, in their structural
forms, rising higher and higher in grades, have been
both prophecy and prelude of the coming man.

The decomposition of rocks is not simply a
chemical death, but a prelude of a higher life ; the
elements are reduced to soils in order to enter into
higher combinations in living plants, which in turn
are to furnish food for the higher orders in the
animal kingdom.

The elevation and depression, the disruption and
contortion ; the vast overturnings and apparent confusion are but exhibitions of the Divinest order
and benevolent purpose ; the wealth of the world
which had been forming for ages was thus made
accessible to man.

The formation of valleys is the prophecy of the
highest civilization ; were man compelled to live

in the mountains, he must forever remain a savage. The storms and wild winds that howled through the forgotten centuries, and the gloomy, glacial rivers that triturated the mountains and smoothed their sides and formed the soils for the homes of the grasses and forests; these forests were buried alive and slept in their tombs for ages, to be packed in a small compass for the uses of man.

When all was ready, man made his advent as the head of creation, the fulfillment of all the promises of the past. He could not have appeared sooner; he could not have lived in the coal period without lungs so constructed as to breath carbonic acid gas; nor in the age of the saurians unless he were a salamander.

Earth must cool off, the climate must change and the atmosphere become purified; this could only be done through ages of mighty revolutions; deaths and burials and resurrections are but processes of developments, not consequents of transgressions.

This globe was not twisted and contorted and thrown into spasms by any event that took place in Eden. The earth is related to other systems of planets, and her great physical revolutions are literal catastrophes; events related to the stars; antagonistic forces, born in the starry worlds, have produced the great convulsions which threw the old seas out of their beds and lifted the great mountain systems from their former homes. The movement of the equinoctial points seems to be the method of the Great Architect in producing these changes.

The revolution of the equinox once in twenty-six thousand years, giving birth to great tides once in ten thousand years, by which all the water was lifted to one side of the globe, and the extremes of heat and cold, are alone sufficient to account for the general cataclysms; among all the generalizations of the facts within the range of the human mind, this seems the most rational.

It is an astronomical fact that man made his advent when the earth began its equinoctial cycle, and that he could not have lived upon the earth sooner, is demonstrable.

That the earth was unfit for the home of man sooner, and that the earth is still unfit for his highest development, may be shown by the fact that man is now limited by certain geographical lines.

Man and the dog may live in almost any climate now known upon the earth. But man can only be developed between fixed lines of latitude. The most complete men and highest civilizations are limited to the best climates. Nations began in, and were limited to, the valleys; they moved west, but were bounded by a narrow belt of latitude, for it was impossible for man to be developed north or south of fixed lines. A Plato could not have been born in Patagonia, nor a Bacon have been produced among the Bushmen.

The highest civilization, the philosopher, prophet and poet, are limited to geographical lines; mind has its zones, the spiritual powers are accelerated or retarded by the influences that flow into the soul from all sides; the relation of matter to mind is not one of cause and effect, but of antecedent and consequent, of action and reaction; a Divine method of the development of man.

Mind both east and west has been colored by the climate; it is seen in the songs of the poets, the formula of the philosopher, and the metaphors of the prophet. Homer revealed a world of beauty in terms of the landscape; the literature of a people is the key to the influence that nature has over mind; neither Solon nor Socrates, David nor Milton, were possible south of the equator; the richest sayings of Hugh Miller are but soul-pictures photographed by the stony hills of Cromarty.

"The banks and braes and streams around the castle of Montgomery"

inspired Burns to sing of his "Highland Mary" in notes as sweet and fragrant as "the hawthorn blossom."

The sweetest songs of our own Bryant are but children of the woods, and fragrant with the odors of the forests of Berkshire. The weird "Poet of the Sierras" must be a Californian. The great teachers were all neighbors; Brahma and Buddha, Confucius and the oriental masters, Moses, Plato and Paul, were all born and developed in the same climate.

Therefore, material conditions are essential to human development. The highest civilization and the most complete specimens of manhood are not yet possible. The earth is still unmatured; three hundred volcanoes, desolating tornadoes, mysterious epidemics, are evidences of its incompleteness. If God took ages to fit the earth to produce a blade of grass, are not long years needed to perfect the highest being? Man is the last order of being and the highest possible, but is not yet complete. Then why expect peace on earth and good will to men in this unfinished state of things?

The distance between the masses and the models of the race is still very great, and the distance between the best models of the race and the Ideal-Man is still greater; but God has a method to shorten that distance by a change of environment.

EVOLUTION AND ENVIRONMENT.

The environments of man set limits to his development and make necessities seem imperfections. The immature condition of the earth, the birthplace and present abode of man, is not the cause but the occasion of all the apparent defects in his history.

The slow development of vegetable and animal life is linked with the slow development of the earth in the history of the past. Life could not advance faster than the adaptation of the climate, which was essential to the various forms of being. The character of the crust of the earth was the special condition of all life, and the climate fixed the grade of being, and the soil and climate still fix the bounds of civilization and the limits to human development.

The earth is still undergoing changes; many forms of life have perished; the extinct races could no more live to-day than man could have existed in the long-forgotten ages; the swamps are still a laboratory of diseases, the air is full of pestilence and dreadful epidemics; the sun has its spots and the solar system is but struggling into harmonious being, necessary to the higher development of man.

Creation is a Divine process, moving onward by a fixed law, according to a perfect plan; man must wait till God completes his work, before he can either interpret or criticize his plans; each man should be God's coadjutor in carrying forward this Divine scheme of human perfection. Man has reached his greatest perfection during the present century, chiefly because his environment has been the most favorable.

But perfection is impossible in a world like this, and in due time changes will come which will create a great epoch in human history. This earth is but a laboratory where the Divine Chemist is completing his methods concerning man; antagonistic

elements will destroy the earth by spontaneous
combustion, but man, with a new and more complete organization than is possible to a world of
gross matter, will live in a state of eternal progression toward the perfection of Deity.

Man is a citizen of the universe; he is not
limited to one planet or one system of suns. He is
limited only by his environment; he is endowed
with capabilities to become a partaker of the Divine
nature. Perfection belongs to God alone, but man
is created in his image. The Gospel and science
are progressive systems of truth to meet the wants
of men in all ages. The evolution of truth keeps
pace with the evolutions of worlds. Eternal progression is the plan of God.

As the history of the evolution of nations shows
development in a special direction, so the limits
of progress were fixed by their environment.
Egypt in its intellectual development drifted
toward science; Greece toward art and literature;
Rome toward law; and Israel toward religion.
Their environments were different, hence thought
developed in these different directions. The environments of this age could produce none of the
old civilizations. The progressive drift of man has

been in the realm of spiritual truth, which, like the tides of the equinox, have ebbed and flowed as they were related to the changes going on in the planetary systems of which man is an important factor.

Israel is the father of our present civilization. The inspiration of David's immortal lyre still thrills the soul of this century; the glories of Solomon will never again be duplicated by any people; this pilgrim nation fills the nooks and corners of the earth, but retains its character.

The Catholic Church was organized with Christ as the head, and retained the doctrines and teachings of the Apostles, and crystalized truth into ecclesiastical forms. This Church was filled with the missionary spirit, and their heroes have never been surpassed; they took possession of every land, and by voluntary sacrifices planted the cross in the uttermost parts of the earth. This organization is the most complete ever known upon the earth, and has its mission among men. But mind, like climate, changes; some new thought turns whole generations, as a pebble turns the course of the stream.

Environments gave birth to a Luther. The Reformation was a great, forward, spiritual movement, a great moral force which threw itself against the mightiest of organizations.

Luther was the spiritual incarnation of his age; he represented a new generation of free thought; and his collision with Catholicism was the collision of the century with the organized centuries of the past.

Who can estimate the results of the shock? It was a mighty spiritual revolution, doing for mind what geological revolutions did for soils and precious metals; it brought great possibilities in the range of all civilized men. It broke the doctrine of centralization of power into fragments; decentralization built up organizations of a hundred creeds, and the race moved up by the law of antagonistic forces to a higher plain.

Deity rallies all the forces and makes nations and churches and leaders of men all his co-laborers, and progress is as rapid as the environment will permit; but the progress leaves behind the gross and material, and the advance is toward the spiritual. As the planet becomes more perfect, the race will improve. Who can estimate the evolution of mind and the development of men and nations and churches, in the coming centuries? Onward!

upward, is the law of the race as it moves forward
toward the millennium, and a matured earth.

Then shall physical catastrophes cease and moral
reforms be accomplished ; then the volcano and
earthquake, the cyclone and the pitiless storm
shall be unknown ; epidemic and pestilence will
cease with the extremes of temperature and a
purified atmosphere ; the vegetable and animal
life will be more complete. Intemperance, re-
venge, treachery and selfishness, the moral diseases of the race, will flee before the reformer,
as pestilence and epidemics flee before a maturing
planet. Creeds, social problems, political plat-
forms, will find a common ground of adjustment,
and peace and good-will prevail. The cause that
will produce the millennium glory, the golden age
so long looked for, is the Supreme Superintendent
of all the forces of the earth, adjusting them all in
the highest interests of man. But the occasion of
peace on earth and good-will to men, is the result of
the change of man's environment ; the Divine
maturing and perfecting the physical world, by
which only such a result becomes possible ; this
is the only, rational solution of the great, unsolved
problem of suffering and wrong.

THE EVOLUTION OF THE SOUL IN SLEEP.

" We are such stuff
As *dreams* are made of, and our little life
Is rounded with a sleep. "   —SHAKESPEARE.

Dream-land has not been completely explored; the survey has been but partial and the field notes imperfect.

The value of sleep to man is spiritualˉ rather than physical; it is more than bodily rest, it is spiritual development, an evolution of the soul, or highest man.

Sleep is a spiritual mystery; a phenomenon of all kinds of life, from the anxious man to the restless fish, all have their times for sleep; even the flowers seem to close their petals and retire from the din and bustle of this noisy world. Sleep involves the relation of the physical to the spiritual.

The spiritual withdraws itself from the outer world and takes up its abode in the nerve centers, where it is nourished and fed from the innumerable, little protoplastic cells which contain all the vital forces of the body; sleep, then, is the spiritual nature retiring from the activities of the body for its own refreshment.

In this state the soul is cut off from the material

world and permitted to explore unfettered, the spiritual world, and often feeds on sunlight administered by angel hands.

All voluntary action with the outer world is suspended; the senses are closed, and all objective life ceases; the soul retreats into the subjective world, a realm of unconsciousness to our waking state; but mind is never so fully awake as when in sleep. "I slept, but my heart was waking," is the highest formulation of this mysterious phenomenon of life.

There is a background to our being; a realm of mystery from whence comes strange thoughts, formulated in images and symbols, which often are untranslatable and unlawful to utter. A sensorium of the invisible; a higher consciousness; an opening up of the powers of the understanding; revelations of the soul expressed in enigmatical symbols. Dreams indicate the moral state of the soul, and have an ethical value; here man's character is often revealed in the presence of his higher self. Sleeping, and dreaming, and visions, are keys to the invisible working of the soul, when it is cut off from the physical body—a method of spiritual evolution and personal development.

DEATH A SPIRITUAL EVOLUTION.

Death is a part of the great plan of Jehovah, a great factor in the evolution and perfection of the spiritual man; an event necessary in the forward march of the centuries and the final development of the race. Man could not become perfect, as the image of his Creator, so long as he was related to gross matter; if he were to live in a physical world for the purpose of discipline, then he must have a physical body suited to his condition; but perfection could not be attained while the spiritual man was fettered by the physical body.

As his material environment changed and became more complete, the generations were more and more developed; but the greatest possible advance must come through the preservation of the best specimens produced; so death was essential as a part of the history of man upon the earth; the lowest forms of character must be developed, while the highest must be perpetuated; but death has its compensation by the law of equivalence in another life.

What is death? It is a spiritual evolution by which the soul is released from all material

environments and united with a spiritual body, for
the purpose of a complete perfection by an eternal
progression toward the Deity, in a spiritual world.

When the protoplasm has been impoverished
and is unable to supply the wants of the spiritual
principle, separation takes place between matter
and spirit, in which gross matter is left, and there
is elaborated from the spiritual organization the
inner soul essence which distinguishes man from
the animal.

Hence death is that change of environment, when
the soul drops gross matter and, united with a
spiritual body, becomes a more perfect organization, fitted for a spiritual environment, for the
spirit leaves the gross matter and takes on an independent existence, and is guided by the inner soul
essence in the higher spiritual spheres.

What, then, is immortality ? The essence of the
soul is identical with the Divine Spirit, and man
becomes a partaker of the Divine nature ; it is this
nature that gives man immortality ; the conscious
relationship with the Divine Spirit. This spiritual
body or environment of the soul, is what Paul
recognizes when he says, there is a natural body
and a spiritual body ; the soul, then, has a spirit-

ual, historical evolution in death by the antagonistic force of a Divine law. Man looses by
this evolution his physical nature, circulation,
digestion, reproduction and sex. He retains all
his spiritual nature, reason, responsibility, consciousness and conscience, personality and personal
identity.

This ethereal being becomes an inhabitant of
the spiritual universe, but is subject to the great
law of environment. Perfect order prevails, and
development follows the same mathematical law in
both worlds.

This development of the soul through the spiritual organization, is the crowning work of Deity on
this planet. All agencies and forces center in the
spiritual development of man. It is the only true
philosophy of the existence and wonderful phenomena of vegetable and animal life; and the
marvelous history of nations and of men. The
past is but a partial revelation of the Divine plan ;
only stations in the forward movements for the
development of man, and the final evolution of the
human soul. This new organization makes man
immortal by his very structure, being a partaker of
the Divine nature.

EVOLUTION AFTER DEATH.

Death is the Key to the Secret Vault. Man's treasure depends upon his conduct in this life. His environment and the character he has formed by his own acts not only determines his condition here, but also the place in the sphere which he enters upon in another life, according to the law of equivalence.

Death is but a passport to a higher state of being, but the condition of the soul in the world beyond is fixed by the law of equivalence; there man enters into a sphere of being which he has made for himself by his conduct in this life; for the measure of character in all worlds is by the universal rule—"According to his works."

Life here is not a vain pursuit after the treasures that lie beyond death, treasures locked up in that Secret Vault; but all real effort is a method of development.

THE LAW OF EQUIVALENCE IS THE LAW OF THE SPIRIT-WORLD.

This world is but little more than a dream of happiness and the pursuit of shadows, that ever elude our grasp and mock our best efforts of energy and skill.

Wealth, fame and pleasure, when obtained can not be transmuted into happiness; for happiness depends on character, and character is related to the life-beyond. While man's environments here have much to do in the development of his life, his innate powers and capabilities, when properly used, are factors in modifying his condition and determining his character, and often change his surroundings. Man is accountable in all conditions of being, for the use or abuse of the talents God has committed to his trust; no responsible being can stand justified short of doing his whole duty, which is determined by obedience to an enlightened conscience; for duty to God and duty to man are identical.

Wealth, is presumed by the majority of the race to be the Key to the Secret Vault. The pursuit of wealth is our age-characteristic. We are a race of gold-hunters; culture and scholarship, art and religion and science, ambition, and even pleasure, are all sacrificed for wealth; business before pleasure, has become a proverb.

The mercantile spirit is the spirit of the century;

our material prosperity has outstripped all the
peoples of the past, and our grandest enterprises
are but the incarnation of this spirit of the age;
time and talent, home and heaven, are sacrificed to
the goddess of wealth. She is presumed to possess
the Key to the Secret Vault. Money may be transmuted into magnificent grounds, palatial residences,
elegant appointments and splendid equipages, but
alas! how often disappointment and despair inhabit
these homes of luxury, and wealth becomes a curse
instead of a blessing. When fortunes are made in
a day by dishonest methods, and man sacrifices
manhood for a treasure that rust will devour and
thieves steal, wealth is an allurement and self-
destructive. Stock-boards and professional gamb-
ling, and lottery schemes, and real estate booms,
are all methods of double dealing. Fortunes obtained by fraud and falsehood are not only a curse
but a crime; not a treasure laid up in the Secret
Vault, but the despoiling of the most valuable
goods ever entrusted to man by the Proprietor of
the universe; it is overdrawing the account of the
future, by the extravagant and criminal expendi-
ture of talent, which ought to have been wisely
invested in the present for future use; it is a per-

version of capabilities and a misuse of the powers
of being, powers and endowments which are the
chief capital to be invested in the spirit-world;
such a misuse of capabilities as compel the soul
to enter a lower place in the sphere of being, beg-
gared and poor indeed ; with infinite obligations
and nothing with which to pay. The real wealth
of all worlds is character ; this is the treasure that
never fades, the reserve fund, locked up in the
Secret Vault of the spirit-world.

Ambition, dreams of this key to happiness and
fame offers to open the treasure-house, but the
price demanded also overdraws the accounts of
the future ; this investment is also a dangerous
risk, a deception, and the proposal is a wicked,
heartless fraud. The glory of earthly crowns and
the blasonry of the victor on the battle-field;
triumphant arches, and the shouts of admiring
multitudes, and monuments of marble, are not
marketable in the spirit-world, where manhood is
the standard of values. By the law of equivalence,
which is the same for all states of being, the
proudest and most victorious despot may surrender himself to the wine-cup and cancel all his
glory by the perversion of his own powers. The

dreams of the man of destiny may be defeated by a rain-storm, and a single night may be the hinge on which may turn the future centuries; the historic field of Waterloo can only be interpreted by the dreary solitudes of St. Helena. The immortal victories which filled Rome with the treasures of the world's spoiler, are linked with the bloody assassination of the mightiest chieftain.

Dom Pedro may retire at night with imperial pride and apparent safety, and the treasure of empire at command; but to-morrow his kingdom is gone, and the king himself becomes an exile in a day; his defenses are his weaknesses; his guards his enemies; his treasures are gone and he a bankrupt; but if the exile be a man, and character remain undimmed, then all the treasures of the Secret Vault are his, and he is rich beyond measure, though he be the synonym of poverty.

Moral worth excels all earthly thoughts of treasure, as eternity excels the fleeting movements of time.

"Lay up treasures in heaven," is the instruction of the Divine Teacher, with an emphasis that rings through the ages, setting forth the importance of moral values. What is moral wealth but the fruits

of a willing obedience to an enlightened conscience ? The fruits of the voluntary acts of kindness and charity to our fellow-man. Acts of mercy,
kindness, charity and spontaneous deeds, spring-
ing from unselfish motives, are the treasures that
never grow old, and that are deposited in the
Secret Vault, where they bear interest forever.

Deeds are the exponents of character ; the real
wealth of the soul ; deposits made for the future ;
not notions, beliefs, resolutions or professions, but
unselfish, spontaneous action in the interest of
others. These are the permanent investments,
secured by the immutable word of the Proprietor
of the universe.

A standard of morality is an essential in the
development of the race, and the formation of
personal character. The state, the church and
the home are responsible for the instruction and
example that shall shape the moral character of
the coming generations. The Ten Commandments,
the Sermon on the Mount, the rest day, and the
doctrines of love and mercy, truth and charity, are
universal truths, that are the common heritage of
the race, and of all men alike ; they are inalienable,
and must not be interfered with by church or state,

Protestant, Catholic, or skeptic ; for the perpetuity of the nation, and the future inheritance of all men alike, depend upon moral character, which is the result of moral training.

The great majority of the children of the state get no moral discipline at home, hence the duty of the state is to fix a moral standard and provide moral instruction for the future citizen ; the state is the guardian of the constitutional rights of the citizen, and all the machinery of the government should be in the interests of the individual. The doctrine of the Republic is, man is greater than the constitution and greater than the state ; the individual right of the citizen is the foundation of all good government ; but the citizen has moral rights as well as political privileges, and the nation is organized to secure these rights ; for the perpetuity and usefulness of the government depends on the rectitude and character of her citizens. The nation should have a conscience and a moral code, as well as a constitution, in order to meet all the wants of the citizen.

The American citizen is supposed to believe in "the Supreme Judge of the world." No man should be eligible to any office in the gift of the people, who does not appeal to "the Supreme Judge of the world" for the rectitude of his intentions. The nation is supposed to believe in a personal God, who superintends the affairs of the world and watches over the interests of the state with a Providential care, and hence proclamations for days of thanksgiving and public worship. The nation believes in prayer, and has made provision for chaplains both in the army and halls of legislation; she believes in the Christian Sabbath, and has set apart one day in seven in which all are relieved from the duties of public offices; and the American Sabbath is a day in which no legal work can be done by the state, and on which every American citizen is entitled to rest from all secular employment.

The nation believes in the Bible; and administers the oath of office to the President and Supreme Judges, and others, with the hand resting upon it. Therefore, it is not only the right, but the sacred duty for the nation to see that the rising generations be instructed in the morals of the state, and Congressional action should make provision for the moral instruction of the future citizen of the state, in her public schools and colleges. The state has

the same right to provide a text-book in morals, as
in arithmetic or grammar; and she is culpable if
she does not discharge this sacred duty; for intelligence without morality is a political evil, that
sooner or later will destroy the best civilization
and transmute the citizen into the savage.

PROGRESSION—THE DIVINE METHOD OF EVOLUTION IN THE FUTURE.

Whatever may have been man's defects, the
history of the race has been one of progression.
The history of the future life will be the same, for
man by his endowment and environment is a
progressive being. The future is not a second
probation or a test of character by trials, but a
development of innate powers under more favorable opportunities; neither is it a world where
man is to be purified by punishment; though
penalties are essential to the administration of
good government and for the higher development
of man, suffering with moral beings must be voluntary, and hence cannot partake of the nature of
punishment; but is a Divine method of development.

The future affords to man a more favorable

environment; being clothed with a spiritual body, and being released from the embarrassment of gross matter; so that under the Divine Superintendency every man moves forward forever, from the grade in which death leaves him, through vast cycles of being toward the perfection of Deity. But the condition in which man enters the future at death, depends upon the use he has made of his powers and the character he formed in his physical environment; so that any loss sustained in this world by failure of duty dwarfs the powers and is eternal loss in all worlds; the law of progress and perfection is immutable—no individual progress without personal effort; so that each determines for himself his grade in the spirit-world.

Work, activity, using the powers with which God has endowed us, is the only method of development, or law of progression. Those that entered the spirit-life in infancy and youth, are to be developed in this new sphere of being without loss; the law of equivalence provides for all apparent disadvantages.

The work of the spirit-land is a ministration of love; the strong help the weak, the wise instruct the ignorant, the good assist the bad; they are all ministering spirits. There seems to be universal sympathy existing among all grades of spiritual being; a fellowship expressing itself in works of benevolence, and methods of helping each other.

Works of mercy are the highest expression of pure, spiritual life known in the highest realms of being; helping others is the chief employment of spiritual beings in all worlds, and the only law of progress revealed. Some are sent from the higher spheres and far-off worlds of light, who have spent ages in this Divine method of progression; they come to lift their fellows to greater hights, and by this process lift themselves. As in mathematics, so in morals, development is in the ratio of duty; light, attraction, chemical combinations and morals are all governed by mathematical law. The same law of evolution is true for all spheres, development by antagonisms; progress is in the ratio of improved opportunities, and the law of compensation where there has been a lack of opportunity; thus man moves on and on! forward and upward, from sphere to sphere, through countless worlds of light, ever progressing toward the infinite perfection of God. Eternal evolution, by the Divine method, is the immutable law of all worlds.

SELFISHNESS, THE ACTIVE, OUTWARD EXPRESSION OF THE LAW OF ANTAGONISM.

Selfishness is not the opposing force in the spiritual universe ; the opposite pole and counter current of all good. It is the natural instinct of all created being, born in us, and is a part of our natural endowment.

Each being is the chief object of interest to its own self ; the grand center about which all else is presumed to revolve.

This great law seems to cast its shadow on all existences ; the animal and vegetable kingdoms are exponents of the law. The strong oppress the weak ; the cruel, armed with weapons of destruction, slay the defenseless ; the powerful are merciless, and the wise and cunning outwit the simple and stupid ; self is the ruling passion of all the animal world.

The history of the animal kingdom is but an exposition of selfish instincts ; birds and beasts, reptiles and insects, are demonstrations of the law.

The shadow falls on the vegetable world. The poisonous plants emit their noxious exhalations and destroy all their neighbors.

The deadly Upas lives alone, because it lives for

self; within the range of its poisonous influence, nothing can exist.

The Canada thistle asserts its right to the soil and is more difficult to dispose of than the Irish land question.

The May weed claims the sunny South for its home and dwells among the aristocrats in the streets of the chief cities; the gympson has squatted as sovereign of the West, and the mission mustard refuses to surrender in the best valleys of Santa Clara.

When this law expresses itself in man, it is more emphatic and is often called depravity.

Volumes have been written on the origin of thorns and thistles and human meanness; and volumes more on the remedies for these supposed moral diseases; but selfishness is part of ourselves; it is an inheritance, as the color of the hair; man is not responsible for this trait, and nobody is to blame.

There is implanted in man, an antagonistic principle which under the power of the will may cancel selfishness; and here is the basis of man's responsibility. Every man may rise higher and higher by his own effort till the race reaches the Golden Rule.

This rule is the great, spiritual climax of human attainment; the objective point of the nation and the individual.

That man may attain this high moral elevation, is demonstrated by the life of Jesus, the complete model man and the only unselfish Being that ever trod the earth. He lived for others, and taught others how to live.

Selfishness crops out in innocent childhood, in church creeds, in the denominational spirit, and in every phase of human life.

The atmosphere of love is the only remedy for selfishness. Jesus was love incarnate; when he was reviled, he reviled not again. Selfishness had no place in his spirit, hence it never manifested itself in his personal history among the worst of men.

Love is the supreme law of all pure spirits, as gravity is the supreme law of all gross matter.

God is love. Love is the fulfilling of the law.

THE CAPITOL OF THE UNIVERSE, OR HOME OF DEITY.

Where is Our Father's house of many mansions? Thought pushes the question to the farthest limits of imagination; all healthy mind demands an answer. Is there not some place in the great universe, some grand center among the systems of worlds; some capital city, the abode of Deity, from which he superintends all the work of his hands?

Man can have no conception of God without form and place, for he made man after his own image.

Science and discovery have extended the boundaries of the universe, until earth is but a mere speck among the infinite worlds, which move in the measureless domain of Deity.

This throne of the Omnipotent is certainly not in the bounds of our solar system. There are eighteen millions of suns and solar systems revolving round a common center, somewhere in the infinite depths of space, (Warren).

There are single stars which have more attractive force than all the known matter in the universe could account for. Sirius and Vega and other stars are white with the inconceivable velocity at which they are moving through space. Job named this group *Chimah,* a beautiful Chaldaic word which is the Divine key to the influence of these stars upon the earth. The word means, pivot or axle, the central point of turning.

It is now an astronomical fact, demonstrated by a series of independent calculations, confirming the revelation of Job and the poetic insight of the Greeks, that Alcyone, the brightest star in the group, is the great center or axle around which our earth is revolving. M. Madler is the best interpreter of Job; for he has mathematically demonstrated Alcyone to be the luminous hinge in the heavens, on which is turning the solar system. Earth and all her sister planets are moving with a velocity of four hundred and twenty-two thousand miles a day, in an orbit that it will require ages to complete. Man has traveled through space since the days of Eden, and yet he is still among the same stars that Adam saw; for we have not moved through one second of the great arc of the solar system since the world began. Yet Alcyone is not the center of the universe of worlds.

The analysis of the light from these more distant

worlds proves that they all belong to one great system. A ray of light from the star Vega would require forty-five years to reach the earth; a star of the twelfth magnitude could not send a ray of light to earth in less than four thousand years; remoter stars, measured by the velocity of light are six thousand years distant from us. Had a photographer set his camera in one of these remote worlds, to take the garden of Eden in its pristine glory, he must wait till the twentieth century before he could get an impression. Wonderful universe! Yet the spectrum analysis shows, that the laws of light, motion and gravity are the same in all worlds, and that all the sun-systems are a unit. We are flying through space in a temperature two hundred degrees below zero, yet our velocity is so great that our climate is comfortable.

Man, by the help of instruments of his own invention, measures stars billions of miles away; thus aided by science, thought moves on in the illimitable space, till imagination with tired wing rests in the unsurveyed territory, in the center of eighteen millions of sun-systems, where Jehovah, the Superintendent of the universe, dwells; here is the capitol of the King in his glory; the council chamber of God; here Jehovah dwells in light which no man can approach unto; the attributes of truth and love, justice and goodness radiate from his brow, and the golden light floods the universe. He holds the mightiest and remotest stars in his hand, watches the motions of the millions of systems he has created; suns with their planetary hosts; worlds upon worlds flying through trackless space, and vast, unbounded solitudes, each obedient to his will; every planet coming to its meridian without the loss of a thousandth part of a second in ten thousand years; yet this God is the Father of man. Our Father! so mindful of all his creatures, that he hears the young ravens when they cry, and not a sparrow falls to the ground without his notice. He hears the softest whisper of his own children. Here, he who was without beginning first began his work; here he dwells in person, superintending and upholding all things by the word of his power. In the highest heaven, amid the seven golden candlesticks, and the seven churches, and the seven trumpets, he sitteth in the circle of the heavens; he speaketh to all his children, saying—

ALL MINE IS THINE !

RECAPITULATION.

1. God created matter out of what was not matter, according to our test, or measurement—the seen came out of the unseen.

2. Creation and planet-formation were necessary, that Deity might give expression to his thoughts and emotions.

3. Earth must take its place in a system of planets before it could be endowed with any life-giving properties.

4. The force, called gravity, was necessary to keep the sun from robbing the earth of all vitality and productive power.

5. This unlimited force, called gravity, is the persistent will power of Deity.

6. All mineral, vegetable and animal evolution is governed by mathematical law; all chemical forms, musical harmony, planetary motions, moral and spiritual development, are all governed by this universal law; the basic principle of mathematics is truth, and truth is an attribute of God.

7.   All the apparent failures we see in the world are due to a partially and imperfectly developed planet, in its relation to our solar system, which affects its environments.

8.   All vegetable and animal life, the evolution of national and personal character, are determined by their environments.

9.   Man never fell from a higher state of perfection, but his history has ever been one of progress according to a Divine plan.

10.   The advance of science, the development of man and the progress of civilization have been in exact ratio of the maturity of the earth and their environment.

11.   The law of antagonism is the Divine method of operation in all nature for the purpose of development; it determines the law of equivalence or compensation, which is universal.

12.   Man's spiritual nature is development from gross matter, under special Divine superintendence.

13.   There is developed from man's spiritual being, by a law of evolution, an inner, soul essence, which distinguishes man from the lower animals. In this inner soul of man God manifests himself and holds communion with his children.

14. All men as well as animals are under Divine law, and are therefore limited, free agents.

15. All the sciences and religious creeds are but agencies under the Divine management in the development of the race.

16. God has given man a perfect pattern, a rule of life, in Jesus the Ideal-Man.

17. The Divine incarnation is not limited to Jesus, for God dwells in all his children.

18. The distribution of rewards and punishments is in accordance with the law of exact equivalence.

19. There is in the universe of nature a central unit of intelligence and power from which emanates all the wisdom and force that are manifested.

20. This great center of intelligence and power is God, in whose image and likeness man was created.

21. This center of Divine Intelligence is not located within our solar system, but in the midst of the sun-systems of the universe.

22. The earth and our solar system is but a colony of yesterday's planting, when compared

with the eternity of the fixed stars and other sun-systems, in the midst of which Deity dwells.

23. Man's spiritual nature is organized upon the principle of eternal progression in knowledge and character.

24. Man retains his identity and recognizes his fellow man in the spirit-world.

25. God could not have done any more for man than he has done.

26. Earth is continually changing from gross matter into ethereal essences and spiritual intelligences.

27. God is manifest both in the truth of science and religion, for religion and science are but one.

28. All the power and intelligence manifested in this world are but the expressions of the Divine thought.

29. All the forces in nature are expressed through the law of antagonism, between solar attraction and gravity of the earth.

30. What we *call* Selfishness is but an active, outward expression of the law of antagonism; it is universal and Divine in its origin.

31. No force in nature is lost, but is either used directly or is transmuted into electric agencies and

used in the development of vegetable and animal life, which in man assumes the forms of intelligence, individuality and personality.

32. Man, in all the events of history, and forward movements of civilization and personal development, is a co-worker with God.

33. Relatively, all men are equal, but positively there is no such thing as equality existing among men. Equality is impossible until all environments are the same.

34. The Key to the Secret Vault is death; and our treasure there is just what we have made it, the results of the acts in this life.

35. An enlightened conscience, illuminated by Divine truth, is the safest guide to the highest plain of life.

THE AUTHOR'S VISION.

Being weary, I laid me down upon my lounge in the office and fell into a kind of sleep. In a half waking condition, I thought I was walking in a beautiful garden, through nice, grassy lawns richly embowered and ornamented with beautiful flowers of the most delicate hue and exquisite fragrance.

This garden seemed alive with most beautiful birds of the richest plumage, and while their melodious notes of heavenly music swept through the groves and mingled with the rich, mellow light that made the place sacred and filled every nook with a silent awe. My path led to the foot of a little mound some six or eight feet high; there I was attracted by a spring of water, clear as crystal, in the form of a circle, about six feet in diameter; the water flowed out beneath my feet among the grass; while I stood reflecting and admiring the sparkling fountain, I beheld a beautiful silver trumpet, about eighteen inches long, floating about upon the glassy bosom of the enchanting water.

While wondering at this strange sight, a most

beautiful woman, clad in a pure white robe, with long golden hair playing with the breeze, appeared before me.

With graceful movement she stooped and took up the silver trumpet, and blew one long, loud blast, that was answered by the neighboring hills; at the echo of this strange and beautiful note, innumerable little fish, white as snow and almost transparent, came to the surface of the spring; from their mouths came forth in great numbers, the most beautiful prismatic gems, which floated about and formed themselves in wreaths and crowns of most exquisite beauty, quivering in the light as if filled with spiritual life.

Astounded and charmed by the enchanting beauty, I asked, "What does all this mean?" The beautiful being that blew the trumpet spoke in gentle tones, and said, "This spring of clear water is the symbol of our spiritual life. The trumpet you saw floating upon the water represents our conscience; the white fish that answered to the call of the trumpet, represent acts of kindness and charity to our fellow man; the pearls and gems which formed themselves into wreaths and crowns, are but the legitimate results or fruits of the acts of kindness and charity, which are to deck and crown man in the spirit-world."

I then asked, "Who is this angelic form that stands before me?" With an accent clear and soft, and in rich and impressive tones, never to be forgotten, she replied, "Ah, I am the symbol of Love, that heavenly, spiritual principle that flows down from Our Heavenly Father, speaking to us through our conscience, and assuring us if we obey our conscience in all things we will be rewarded with a crown in the spirit-world."

I then asked if our conscience was the highest authority and best guide to govern us in this world. She paused a moment, then answered, "Yes, an enlightened conscience, with the light that comes from Divine truth, is the surest guide we have in a world like this."

FINIS.

INDEX TO TOPICS.

CPSIA information can be obtained
at www.ICGtesting.com
Printed in the USA
BVHW070823040219
539400BV00034B/2362/P